1001 Things Every Graduate Should Know

(How to succeed in the adult world)

HARRY H. HARRISON JR.

D0954102

NASHVILLE   DALLAS   MEXICO CITY   RIO DE JANEIRO

Table of Contents

1001 Things Every Graduate Should Know

(HOW TO SUCCEED IN THE ADULT WORLD)

Hello.

This is the real world talking.

So you're about to graduate and are counting down the days till you can get out of the house. Your 'rents have become unbearable. Your little sister is a dweeb. Your curfew makes it seem like you're being held hostage. In a few months, you are so gone. You're going to party like they do on MTV. College will be a lay-down, you'll make a million before you're twenty-five, you'll date only A-list members. *Not hot* need not apply.

Oh, there is one tiny little thing you might want to think about. Well, maybe a thousand tiny little things. Like, what do you do when you can do anything you want? And what if there's more to life than it looks like on MTV? There are matters surrounding roommates who smell, choosing the right college classes, and not acting like a social cripple around blondes. There are issues about having to earn money, living in a tiny dorm or apartment, and not maxing out credit cards.

Later come real adult concerns: finding and keeping jobs, unreasonable bosses and people not thinking you're as special as your mother does. It can get so bad you'd want to move back home, except your bedroom is now your little sister's media room. So you're stuck out here with the rest of us.

The good news is, most everything you need to know about the real world is in this book.

True, there are no pictures. On the plus side, however, the sentences are short. And what you read today, you can start using today! So don't put off studying it. The final exam comes quickly. And lasts for the rest of your life.

You Need to Know How to Prepare for College

1. You need to know your ticket to
the upper middle-class is punched
with a college degree.

•

2. You need to know you're not entitled
to a college degree. In fact, you're no
longer entitled to anything.

•

3. You need to know over one-third of
the people who drop out of college do so
because they can't handle the workload.

•

4. You need to know homework,
responsibility, and self-discipline take
on different meanings in college.

•

5. You need to know that everything you thought
in high school—about studying, hard work,
achievement, meeting people, how cool
you were—is all out the window.

6. You need to know it doesn't matter who you were in high school. Nobody cares. But it does matter who you think you are now.

•

7. You need to know how to have an original thought. This ability really helps.

•

8. You need to know that if you've acquired the discipline to keep studying even when you're tired and bored, you can graduate from Harvard early.

9. You need to know to not spend the summer before your freshman year wasted. The smart students already know the first semester's reading assignments and are getting ahead.

•

10. You need to know college is a rough place to learn you're not the center of the universe.

11. You need to know to be reading
something denser than text messages.

•

12. You need to know how to defend your opinions
and values. They will be challenged regularly.

•

13. You need to know how far away
you want to live from Mom and Dad
and your boyfriend. Loneliness is
a big reason kids flame out.

•

14. You need to know going to a school
that's either too large or too small can
result in the same thing—leaving.

•

15. You need to know if a college costs $40,000 a
year and you have limited resources, you'll spend
more time worrying about money than studying.

16. You need to know whether you're ready. There's a lot to be said for taking a year off to work for the Peace Corps or with Doctors Without Borders or even to travel Europe. Do something to stimulate your thought process.

•

17. You need to know taking a year off before you start school won't impact your college admission. In fact, many top-tier schools think it's a great idea.

•

18. You need to know that when your parents said, "You can be anything you want to be," they were humoring you. You were six. You need to find out what you're good at.

•

19. You need to know to take personal responsibility. Success or failure is now based on your decisions and your effort.

20. You need to know when to
turn off the television. This skill pays
dividends your freshman year.

•

21. You need to know the absolute quickest
way to alienate a professor is to complain to the
department chair or dean about a grade.

•

22. You need to know your college classes
will be filled with strange-looking people.
Odds are, you may be one of them.

•

23. You need to know your profs will not
immediately respond to your e-mails. Especially
the ones you send Sunday night about
homework due Monday.

•

24. You need to know that the nerd
in the corner of the library is going to
be running a Fortune 500 company
one day. Make friends.

25. You need to know to find someone
to emulate who isn't in rehab.

•

26. You need to know if you're spending more time
thinking about your tan and your abs than your mind,
you'll be out of school by the end of the year.

•

27. You need to know professors don't
have to get along with you. You have to
learn to get along with them.

•

28. You need to know not to get upset
when college ceases to be fun.

•

29. You need to know to attend freshman
orientation camp—or whatever it's called. Yes, you
will probably sit in some "Kum Ba Yah" circle and
play stupid name games, and you can already tell it
won't be cool, but on the first day of school, you'll
actually know people. And that *is* cool.

30.   You need to know it's time
to start reading biographies of esteemed
politicians, spiritual leaders, and successful
businesspeople. These are the people
you want to be like.

•

31.   You need to know you're more
likely to finish your degree faster if
you start at a small private college
instead of at a state school.

•

32.   You need to know small private
colleges look more expensive, but they often
come with more grants, scholarships, and
loans than state schools do.

•

33.   You need to know it takes longer to graduate
from a large state university—sometimes six
years—because some required classes
have a one-year waiting list.

34.   You need to know two words
if you have no idea what you want to
do in five years: liberal arts.

•

35.   You need to know the whole point
of college: better job opportunities.

•

36.   You need to know that if you pick a
college with 200 kids per class, you can get
emotionally, mentally, and physically lost.

•

37.   You need to know the worst reason to choose
a school is because your high-school flame is going
there. The odds are high that one of you will leave.

•

38.   You need to know that every year
you dally in college is one year of full-time
income you lose in the job market. That
makes college even more expensive.

39. You need to know it doesn't matter if you go to a big college or a small college if your head isn't screwed on straight. You'll be out in a year.

•

40. You need to know that few freshmen are prepared for the amount of work college demands outside of class.

•

41. You need to know to register for fifteen hours per term. That's a full load but not impossible, and if you have to drop a class, you won't go into academic probation or become financially ineligible.

42. You need to know you can
buy software—the really good stuff—at dirt
cheap student prices. Check Apple.com or
AcademicSuperstore.com.

•

**43. You need to know the least important thing
on campus is a car. Thousands and thousands of
students survive without one.**

•

44. You need to know the first
semester is the hardest.

You Need to Know Your Roommate Might Smell

45. You need to know to send in your dorm reservation as soon as you get accepted. On-campus housing fills up quickly.

•

46. You need to know to live in the dorm. It's the easiest way to make friends, feel connected to the school, and avoid flunking out.

•

47. You need to know you're moving into a dorm built fifty years ago, not a condo built last week.

•

48. You need to know all your clothes, pillows, quilts, towels, medicine, grooming aids, hair products, blankets, sheets, radio, computer, TV, shoes, and minibar have to fit into a space the size of a MINI Cooper.

•

49. You need to know your roommate will probably never be your best friend. That's okay. Your friends don't want to live with you.

50. You need to know you won't have a private bathroom. In fact, you could share a bathroom with twenty or so people.

•

51. You need to know the most important shower accessory is a pair of Crocs or flip-flops. What's living on those floors can stop an army.

•

52. You need to know to not worry whether or not your roommate likes you. Find reasons to like your roommate.

•

53. You need to know kids who live in the dorms make higher grades.

•

54. You need to know a dorm is the cheapest housing around for miles. Unaffordable housing means you have to work part-time jobs longer just to afford a roof over your head.

55.   You need to know you can't change anybody by getting mad or arguing. Even if that person sleeps three feet above you.

•

56.   You need to know husbands and wives fight, brothers and sisters fight, and roommates fight. Don't let a misunderstanding bring you home.

•

57.   You need to know that, in many states, if you get into a fistfight with your roommate, you can be charged with domestic violence. Weird, but true.

•

58.   You need to know whether you and your roommate need rules. Like rules about borrowing makeup, playing Halo 3 at 4 a.m., passing gas more than three times an hour. Rules help with these things.

•

59.   You need to know it takes about three months to adjust to dorm life.

60.   You need to know to go to your
RA (resident assistant) if your roommate
is from hell. In extreme cases, colleges
will move you around.

•

61.   You need to know applying the Golden
Rule helps immensely with roommates.

•

62.   You need to know to lock your
room when you go down the hall
to pee. Even at night.

•

63.   You need to know your roommate may
not share your fondness for Puff Daddy
or Twisted Sister. Pack your iPod.

You Need to Know
the First Two Weeks
Help Determine the
Next Four Years

64. You need to know the more people
you meet in the first couple of weeks,
the greater your chances of staying put
and getting your degree.

•

65. You need to know meeting people is never
easier than during your first fourteen days.
Everybody is anxious to make friends.

•

66. You need to know that who your
friends are will have a direct influence
on your success at college.

•

67. You need to know that the good-looking
blonde sitting beside you is shy
too. Introduce yourself.

•

68. You need to know there's no way you can look
any stupider in class than the other freshmen.
Unless you show up in your pajamas.
Then you'll look stupider.

69. You need to know college isn't as easy as it seems the first week. Start studying now or you'll be three chapters behind by the second week.

•

70. You need to know to start getting As quickly.

•

71. You need to know the lines at the bookstore will stretch to China the first two or three days. This is not an excuse for showing up in class without books. It's a reason to show up at the bookstore early.

•

72. You need to know to make friends in your classes. It helps to have people to compare notes with.

•

73. You need to know the school makes a lot of money off freshmen who park illegally in order to get to class on time.

74. You need to know where your classes are before school starts. This small gesture says, "Hey, I have a brain and I'm using it!"

•

75. You need to know to not schedule back-to-back classes a half-mile apart.

•

76. You need to know that professors will post the semester's reading assignments, term papers, and exams online and/or hand them out in class. This gold mine of information is called a syllabus. Make a copy. Send it to your mother. Guard it with your life.

•

77. You need to know that a syllabus isn't a list of suggestions.

•

78. You need to know the "I didn't know it was due" excuse that might have worked in high school won't work now. Really. Don't try it. You'll be laughed out of class.

79. You need to know that the dates assigned for exams and papers are what you now plan your life around.

•

80. You need to know that if a class is too full for you to get into, attend the first class anyway. The professor just might squeeze you in.

•

81. You need to know the newfound freedom that college offers will either make you or break you.

•

82. You need to know how to get yourself organized. The way you spend your time and energy will have a direct impact on whether or not you make it to your sophomore year.

•

83. You need to know being on time will keep you in college. Be on time to class, with your assignments, with your reading, with your papers, with your forms, with your tuition checks.

84. You need to know the rules: what gets you thrown out of a dorm; what you need to do to graduate; what behavior is acceptable and what isn't. It's all there in your student handbook.

•

85. You need to know to meet with your counselor two times a semester. That person is paid to advise you on what major to pursue, tell you what classes to take and to drop, and help you resolve scheduling conflicts.

•

86. You need to know to call your counselor before you call your parents. In fact, you probably won't be able to reach your parents. They're off working second jobs to pay for college.

•

87. You need to know to not make the mistake of thinking that since you've gone to class, you're done for the day. You're really just starting.

88.   You need to know even a party school means lots of homework. Yes, it's called false advertising.

•

89.   You need to know to visit the financial aid office and apply for grants or loans for the next semester even if you don't think you qualify. You never know.

•

90.   You need to know the biggest mistake most students make is to not take advantage of their school's resources. Your tuition pays for all the health services, study assistance programs, tutors, career guidance officers, and other campus professionals. Use them.

•

91.   You need to know to find a place for studying. It could be Starbucks. Or behind the stacks at the college library. Or your dorm room. You need a place where your brain realizes it's time to get serious.

•

92.   You need to know it's important to develop a relationship with your professor now, not a week before exams and you're not sure what a cosine is.

93. You need to know to develop a balance between studying and playing, sleeping and exercising, meeting new people and forming relationships. Kids who keep everything in balance wind up with degrees.

•

94. You need to know to join a study group. You'll meet people—and some studying might actually break out.

•

95. You need to know that studying is job #1.

•

96. You need to know the nerds win in the end.

You Need to Know Choosing a Major Is More Crucial to Future Financial Success Than Choosing a College

97. You need to know that choosing the right major is often the key to getting the preferred internships, gaining admittance into the highest-rated graduate programs, and landing the highest starting salary in your field.

•

98. You need to know tools like the Myers-Briggs Type Indicator can help point you in the right direction for choosing your major. Talk to someone at the career guidance center.

•

99. You need to know declaring a major will make choosing classes a lot easier.

•

100. You need to know to take a number of different courses to see what you like if you have absolutely no idea what to major in. You may have a latent ability for science and not know it.

101.   You need to know what's going on today
in your fields of interest. Visit career centers, Web
sites, professional journals, career fairs. Talk to
different people in each field.

•

102.   You need to know to not listen to all
that nonsense about college being a time of
"personal exploration." At up to $50,000
a year, it's job training.

•

103.   You need to know to not be afraid to
change your major if you can't pass the required
classes. You may dream of a pre-med degree, but if
your highest grade in biology is 19, you're
never going to be a doctor. Move on.

•

104.   You need to know it's perfectly okay to
check the "undecided" box next to the word
major when you enroll. You have a couple of
years to find the field of study that makes
you want to get up in the morning.

105. You need to know you need to just choose a major and graduate if, by your third year, you have no idea what you want to do. According to a British study, around 40 percent of the jobs available to new graduates are open to people with a degree in any subject.

•

106. You need to know to not let current market conditions dictate your degree choices. What's hot today could be stone-cold in four years. Ask any computer engineer.

•

107. You need to know that one way to decide on a major is to list the degrees you can never in a million years see yourself earning. Now you have a much shorter list to agonize over.

•

108. You need to know that personality, aptitude, interest, and values are as important as a starting salary when you're choosing a major.

109.   You need to know to use summer internships and missionary work to explore degree ideas. Go to Romania with a dental mission team. You may find you love yanking teeth.

•

110.   You need to know to make sure you get an adviser in your major's department and check in regularly. She can help identify those classes that are vital to your degree plan, but are offered only once a year.

•

111.   You need to know that every time you change your major after your junior year, you add at least one year to your graduation date.

You Need to Know
How to Choose Classes

112.   You need to know to take classes that will help you meet your graduation requirements. Forgetting this is why kids spend six years in college and leave with $400-a-month student loan payments—and no degree.

•

113.   You need to know that even liberal arts and philosophy majors can use some business courses.

•

114.   You need to know there are different pathways in each industry. Hollywood has its money people and its creative people, health care has its doctors and administrators, high tech has its engineers and its marketing people.

•

115.   You need to know to ask older students about professors. They are happy to share war stories.

•

116.   You need to know about www.ratemyprofessor.com and www.pickaprof.com. See how other students from your school graded the professors.

117.   You need to know to not pick a professor because he's the funniest person on campus. Pick a prof whose students go on to get great jobs.

•

118.   You need to know that some of your most valuable classes will not be fun. In fact, they will make you want to call your mother. These classes will also, however, be instrumental in getting you into graduate school and then into a great job.

•

119.   You need to know you can't tell what a class covers by its name. In some schools, "Communication 101" refers to a television production class, and in other schools it has to do with speech and hearing problems.

•

120.   You need to know that just because you bombed biology in ninth grade doesn't mean you can't handle biology in college. You'll be amazed at what determination and maturity can do.

You Need to Know How to
Survive Campus Life

121. You need to know to talk to anyone and everyone—to the person waiting outside the lecture hall, sitting in the cafeteria, walking next to you as you cross campus.

•

122. You need to know to not try to impress everyone you meet.

•

123. You need to know your campus bookstore has everything you need to get through your classes. But its prices may rival Neiman Marcus.

•

124. You need to know professors can help you land campus jobs, smooth admission into required classes, and put you back on track when class work begins to kick you in the butt.

•

125. You need to know if your grades are substandard, it's even more critical for you to take advantage of college internships and leadership positions in extracurricular activities.

126. You need to know to watch your language. Anything racist, sexist, or threatening can have you thrown out.

•

127. You need to know it's not okay for professors to hit on you.

•

128. You need to know that your campus computer center contains viruses that could stop the Defense Department's computers. Handle with care.

•

129. You need to know the campus tutoring center is the place to go if you can't figure out a chemistry problem or answer a homework question.

•

130. You need to know the most important office on campus is the registrar's office. They are the people who keep all your academic and personal records and who also determine who graduates when by deciding who takes classes when. Go bearing gifts.

131. You need to know your college offers workshops on everything from speed-reading to writing marketing plans. Take advantage of them. They're cheap, if not free.

•

132. You need to know that your college regularly sponsors lectures by some of the most important people in the world. Attending them is a great way to understand there's more to life than the next kegger.

•

133. You need to know academic clubs like the Biology Club or the Pre-med Club or the Marketing Club are key to meeting contacts who lead to job offers. While your classmates are off suntanning, you can be networking.

•

134. You need to know who, where, and when to turn in your FAFSA (Free Application for Federal Student Aid) forms every year.

135.   You need to know how to contact campus security if you want a late-night escort to your car.

•

136.   You need to know your biorhythms.
Can you function well at 8 a.m., or are you better off starting with a 10 a.m. class?

•

137.   You need to know how to navigate the library search engine. You're going to need things like call numbers, subject headings, etc. You're not in Google anymore.

•

138.   You need to know how to use every tool in the library. Before your first research paper is due.

•

139.   You need to know that you have to enroll for classes every semester. Do it early and you'll get the classes you want. Do it late and your kids may graduate before you do.

140.   You need to know the administration and the faculty's office staff. They're the ones who can find you fifteen minutes on a prof's calendar.

•

141.   You need to know you can form good habits simply by practicing them daily.

•

142.   You need to know to read anything that shows up from the university in your e-mail or mailbox.

•

143.   You need to know a cheap bike is a great way to get around campus without worrying about parking tickets. You'll also be able to get closer to your classrooms.

•

144.   You need to know real-life tragedies happen on campus. You can be assaulted, fall down stairs, be involved in a wreck, get your wallet stolen. Stay aware. And have a plan.

You Need to Know How to
Survive College Classes

145. You need to know to go to class.
Seriously. It's the key to getting a degree.

•

146. You need to know to go to class even if you
don't have your homework done. Or if you're hung
over. Or if you're sick as a dog. Go to class.

•

147. You need to know it's as important to learn
the instructor as it is to learn the material.

•

148. You need to know you'll
see questions on tests not covered
in class. Professors love to see if
you've been reading.

•

149. You need to know the core vocabulary used in
each class. If the professor seems to be speaking a
foreign language, drop the course and take a primer.

•

150. You need to know you could have two
hours of reading tonight. Per class.

151.   You need to know to read your assignments before class. The professor's lecture will make a lot more sense.

•

152.   You need to know the best students don't actually enjoy every minute of studying. They struggle too.

•

153.   You need to know that if you don't really comprehend the fundamentals of what you're studying, call a tutor. Before the final.

•

154.   You need to know that even if an assignment is worth only 1 percent of your grade, you'll be grateful for every single percent you racked up come the end of the semester.

•

155.   You need to know to study your hardest subjects first. Calculus makes even less sense when your brain is tired.

156. You need to know you can do everything right and still get a B from your professor.

•

157. You need to know partial credit beats no credit. Turn in your homework even if it's late.

•

158. You need to know there's a difference between critical thinking and memorization. You can memorize a girl's phone number. Critical thinking is analyzing whether or not she will be seen with you.

•

159. You need to know to address your professor as either "Doctor" or "Professor." Not "Miss." You're no longer in high school.

•

160. You need to know to have an opinion and to share it in class. This tells the professor you're not dead.

161. You need to know professors expect you to complete your assignments on time. They won't argue about a late paper. They'll just fail you.

•

162. You need to know that buckling down and getting your work done takes a lot less time and stress than cramming all night.

•

163. You need to know you're toast if you miss more than one math class.

•

164. You need to know to do all your homework, even if you don't have to turn it in. It's how you learn.

•

165. You need to know professors hate having stupid questions asked in class. They'll think you're trying to be the center of attention.

166.   You need to know some of your assignments won't be due for months. Waiting months to start them, though, will have you in community college next semester.

•

167.   You need to know that getting one of the highest grades in class on a hard college test is one of the coolest experiences you will ever have. And it's totally worth the effort.

•

168.   You need to know to not blame the professor because you're failing.

•

169.   You need to know you can't keep all your assignments—what they are, when they're due—in your head. This is the same head that can't remember that hot blonde's name. And you think you can remember your chemistry assignments? Right . . .

•

170.   You need to know you won't have time for a regular afternoon nap or tanning appointment.

171. You need to know your professor could be an atheist, a communist, a bigot, a feminist, or a sexist. Your job is still to make your grades.

•

172. You need to know which readings in your classes are crucial and which ones are optional. Students who don't know this study the wrong material for hours.

•

173. You need to know you're not entitled to a do-over.

•

174. You need to know to approach class work like a job. Figure out how much time you need to spend on your studies and consistently spend that amount of time on them.

•

175. You need to know to not give up when you learn you're not above average.

176. You need to know college is a lot like the real world: some people can do some things better with less effort.

•

177. You need to know to sit as close to your professor as you can. It's easier for her to start recognizing you.

•

178. You need to know your professors won't praise you for a job well done. They expect you to perform.

•

179. You need to know a B or C is no reason to argue with your professor. See it as a sign you need to work harder.

•

180. You need to know that if you store your homework on a flash drive, you can work on it at the computer center between classes.

•

181. You need to know studying till 3 a.m. isn't unusual.

182. You need to know to go to the library and study between classes. Not go back to bed.

•

183. You need to know that if you've studied hard throughout the day, you can be surfing YouTube at 10 p.m. And still making your grades.

•

184. You need to know to study one subject at a time. Knock out calculus before moving on to English Lit.

•

185. You need to know if you can't get to know the professor, get to know the TA (teaching assistant). You need someone on your side.

•

186. You need to know to not wear flip-flops and gym shorts to class in thirty-degree weather so you can look cool. You'll look hung over. Or stupid.

•

187. You need to know that if you need to see a tutor every week, odds are you've picked the wrong major.

188.   You need to know professors have no interest in helping you if you haven't been coming to class all semester.

•

189.   You need to know to study with someone smarter than you.

•

190.   You need to know there are Web sites that can help you succeed. Freetranslation.com and college-cram.com are some of the cooler ones.

•

191.   You need to know if you're not making As, don't give up. Grad schools and employers like Bs too.

•

192.   You need to know to not get discouraged by your first-semester grades. It takes a while for most students to find their legs.

•

193.   You need to know that you need to actually learn what you were taught in class today. Learn the vocabulary, understand the chart, decipher the equation—don't go back to the dorm until you understand it.

You Need to Know
How to Study

194.   You need to know how you learn. Auditory learners process information differently than kinesthetic learners do. Ask your counseling center to help you figure this out.

•

195.   You need to know that not everything in your textbook is important. Learn when to skim, when to scan, and when to read.

•

196.   You need to know if you're highlighting over 30 percent of a passage, it's time to memorize it.

•

197.   You need to know studying while drinking beer is not studying. It's drinking. And, while it may be fun, you won't remember anything.

•

198.   You need to know if you study at least two hours for every one hour you're in class, your skin will clear up, you'll be infinitely more attractive to the opposite sex, and fame and fortune await.

199. You need to know "later" never comes. Don't put studying off till later.

•

200. You need to know that if you got As in high school without studying, you may not have the study habits to succeed in college.

•

201. You need to know math is learned by doing the problems. Over and over again.

•

202. You need to know that even if you landed on campus with a full scholarship, you're going to have to work harder than ever before to keep it. Full-scholarship students lose their scholarship money all the time.

•

203. You need to know the study habits you develop as a freshman will either benefit you or haunt you for the next four years.

204. You need to know to drink lots of cold water as you're pulling an all-nighter. This will force you to get up and go to the bathroom often. Even if you're getting drowsy.

•

205. You need to know to close your dorm door when you study. An open door says, "Come on in. Let's party."

•

206. You need to know to study with all the lights on. Especially the later it gets.

•

207. You need to know that studying in bed is a great way to wake up really refreshed for the next morning's test. Doomed, but refreshed.

•

208. You need to know that if the rest of the class is four chapters ahead of you, you may want to cancel this weekend's plans. And next weekend's.

209. You need to know how to stay awake: coffee, washing your face ten times a night, studying with a friend. More Red Bull.

•

210. You need to know the A students get ahead on weekends. It's weird what the brain can do when it's not sitting in a smoke-filled bar.

•

211. You need to know to keep a textbook with you at all times. Pull it out while riding the bus, waiting in line, sitting in the doctor's office.

•

212. You need to know that, in contrast to high school, a college class might only have two or three tests all semester. Blow just one and you're, well, on the five-year plan. Then the six-year plan. Then the I'll-come-back-in-ten-years plan.

•

213. You need to know that the professors may not review the material you're going to be tested on. You're expected to know it.

214. You need to know you're toast if you don't read the assignments, if you're only semi-conscious while reading, or if you expect the professor to teach you everything you need to learn. Burnt toast.

•

215. You need to know there's a difference between reviewing a semester's worth of material and cramming a semester's worth of reading into the same period of time.

•

216. You need to know the goal of studying is not memorizing but understanding.

217.   You need to know CliffsNotes help in understanding things like Shakespeare or Voltaire. But you still have to read the stuff.

•

218.   You need to know to set goals. Like doing twenty algebra problems before calling your girlfriend. Or reading and understanding an entire chapter before calling your parents for money. It works.

•

219.   You need to know to concentrate on the text headings as you read a chapter, not skim over them. Test questions often come from those headings.

You Need to Know How to
Read for Content When
There Are No Pictures

220. You need to know how to
find the main idea. Of a textbook.
Or a novel. Or an article.

•

221. You need to know how to
recognize material that will be covered on a test.
Things like highlighted text, questions posed in
margins, diagrams, pictures, and tables. They're all
shouting, "This could be on the test!"

•

222. You need to know the glossary
of terms if you're to have any idea what the
textbook is talking about.

•

223. You need to know that definitions
of key terms may not be on a test, but will be
critical to solving test problems.

•

224. You need to know that literature requires you
to, every now and then, stop and think about what
you're reading. Is the author serious? Is it a satire?
Is it a dream? Do you have any idea?

You Need to Know
How to Take Notes
When You Can Barely
Understand the Professor

225. You need to know taking notes will help you pay attention—which is, of course, the . . . uh . . . point.

•

226. You need to know the Cornell Method for taking notes. Draw a 1 1/2-inch margin on the left. Take notes on the right side of the paper and add questions pertaining to the notes on the left side.

•

227. You need to know to set up a binder for each class you're taking. Mixing economics notes with notes on Voltaire can only lead to academic ruin.

•

228. You need to know to take notes even when you record lectures. If you can't understand the professor in person, there's no way you'll know what he's saying on tape.

•

229. You need to know to file in your binder every day all the class notes, text summary notes, and papers your professor hands out. Do this so you don't lose anything.

230. You need to know to read over
your notes before class starts. Professors
have a way of assuming you're on
the same page with them.

•

231. You need to know that if
your professor says something more
than once, she's all but telling you,
"This will be on the test."

•

232. You need to know to create
headings for each lecture and subheadings
for topics covered throughout. This
makes reviewing your notes at
exam time much easier.

•

233. You need to know to type your
notes on your computer after every class before
you do anything else. Now this information is
filed in your computer, organized for exams,
and possibly implanted in your brain.

234. You need to know to number
and date each page of notes you take.
You also need to know to not try to
write down every word. Put the
lecture in your own words.

•

235. You need to know to leave spaces
between lines and double spaces between
ideas. Your notes will be easier to review later.

•

236. You need to know to
copy down everything your
professor writes on the board.

You Need to Know That College Papers Are Longer Than Half a Page

237.   You need to know nothing says, "Last minute" like a poorly written paper.

•

238.   You need to know to pack *The Elements of Style* by William Strunk Jr. and E. B. White. It's your best hope of getting through freshman comp.

•

239.   You need to know to never write a paper using only Wikipedia. You'll sound just like all the other losers. Besides, half of that stuff is wrong.

•

240.   You need to know that if your paper is not properly footnoted, you're going to fail.

•

241.   You need to know to set up regular conferences with the professor to review your progress. Start early in the semester.

•

242.   You need to know that if your paper doesn't make a point, you're going to fail.

243. You need to know that if
another student has turned in your
paper before, you're going to fail.

•

244. You need to know to finish your paper
at least three days before it's due. That will give
you time to proofread it. Again and again.

•

245. You need to know to read your finished
paper out loud to someone else.

You Need to Know How to Take an Exam without Freezing Up

246. You need to know what pages the test will cover. Many kids fail because they carefully read, memorize, and review the wrong chapters.

•

247. You need to know what type of test you're studying for. Multiple choice? Critical thinking? Essay? It helps to know your format.

•

248. You need to know to not hang with students who are freaking out over the test. Panic is contagious.

•

249. You need to know you're not going to have time to do a semester's worth of reading in one night.

•

250. You need to know there's no time limit on studying. You work as long as it takes you to gain understanding.

251.   You need to know to use your course outline when reviewing the material. It shows you how your professor was thinking when preparing the course. Chances are she'll structure the exam the same way.

•

252.   You need to know the why of what you're studying. Being able to discuss the impact and significance of an event is as important as memorizing dates and facts. Maybe more important.

•

253.   You need to know to start studying at least a week before a test. The A students started even earlier.

•

254.   You need to know to go to the class review sessions. Consider them a gift from your professor.

•

255.   You need to know how to study using a highlighter. But if you highlight the whole book, you will learn nothing.

256. You need to know what works for you. Flash cards, studying with a friend, hiding in the library—learn what helps you learn.

•

257. You need to know to not lie to yourself. Don't tell yourself you know the material when you've only looked at it once.

•

258. You need to know to have someone quiz you. Sometimes this is called a study date. And you actually, well, study.

•

259. You need to know that cramming for tests and exams indicates you've been busy with something other than studying.

•

260. You need to know that if you have headaches and nausea, you're infected with test anxiety. Get up and study.

261. You need to know to get your act together the night before the exam. Don't be running around the next morning looking for pens, calculators, and books.

•

262. You need to know to sleep before an exam. A tired brain means incoherent thinking and writing.

•

263. You need to know to read all of the instructions before you begin taking a test. People who can't be bothered with instructions fail.

•

264. You need to know whether you can make notes on your exam. If you can, write down the most crucial, most-likely-to-forget information as soon as the exam starts.

•

265. You need to know that if you don't know the answer to the first question, don't agonize over it. Move on.

266.   You need to know which
questions count the most and spend
your time on those.

•

267.   You need to know to show
your work or line of reasoning. Even
if you get the answer wrong, you
may get partial credit.

•

268.   You need to know to bring
a watch. Check your progress at
fifteen-minute intervals.

•

269.   You need to know that if the
test is harder than you imagined,
don't panic. Forget getting the A.
Your goal is to survive.

•

270.   You need to know that if other students
are finishing before you, it might well be they've
given up. Take as much time as you can.

271. You need to know it's critical to do well on the first exam. Or you'll be playing catch-up the rest of the semester.

•

272. You need to know the six most common kinds of essay questions—and the kind of organized response they call for: definition, analysis, cause and effect, comparison-contrast, process, thesis and support.

•

273. You need to know to look for key words in an essay question that indicate how you will organize your answer.

•

274. You need to know that spending a few hours at the writing lab can increase your ability to answer essay questions.

You Need to Know How to Take a Multiple-Choice Test without Choosing "B" Every Time

275. You need to know to read the beginning
of each multiple-choice question (called the stem)
together with each possible answer. Sometimes you
can rule out answers because, grammatically, they
don't work with the stem.

·

276. You need to know how to study every
part of the question stem—the subject, the verb,
and the modifiers. That's how you'll understand
what's really being asked.

·

277. You need to know that multiple-choice
tests require more than merely recognizing true
statements. They often require recognizing the
right answer in the context of the question.

278. You need to know that multiple-choice questions sometimes require fine distinctions between correct and nearly correct statements. In other words, memorization won't help. Understanding does.

•

279. You need to know there's no magic in picking "C" if you don't know the answer. It's an urban myth.

•

280. You need to know sometimes a multiple-choice answer is so obvious you'll think it's wrong. Especially if you've been studying and you know the material.

281.   You need to know to do the
multiple-choice part of a test first. It can
hold clues to the other exam questions.

•

282.   You need to know whether you'll be
marked down for an incorrect answer. If not, it
pays to guess. If you are penalized, answer
only the questions you know.

•

283.   You need to know to answer the
easiest questions first. Then go back
and work on the harder ones.

•

284.   You need to know a trick for dealing with
multiple-choice tests: eliminate the obviously
wrong answers first. Then concentrate on choosing
between the correct and almost-correct answers.

285.   You need to know words
such as *every, all, none, always,* and
never indicate the correct answer must
be an undisputed fact.

•

286.   You need to know that, in the
social sciences, absolutes are rare.

•

287.   You need to know that words like *usually,*
often, generally, may, and *seldom* are qualifiers that
could indicate a true statement.

•

288.   You should know subheads
from the textbook frequently show
up in the questions, either in the
stem or as the right answer.

289. You need to know to do an analysis of each test after you get your grade. Figure out why you missed certain questions.

•

290. You need to know that, on multiple-choice tests, the answer may indeed always be "B." Professors like to do that.

You Need to Know
Cheating and Plagiarism
Can Get You Kicked Out
. . . No Matter How Much
Your Mother Complains

291. You need to know to bring
your character into the classroom.

•

292. You need to know that
copying something without attribution,
even if you find it on some Russian
Web site, is plagiarism.

•

293. You need to know that unless
the professor tells you otherwise,
sharing information is cheating.

•

294. You need to know to not turn in
any paper you yourself didn't write.

295. You need to know that if a high grade is important enough to sell your soul, it should be important enough to miss a party or two, stay up a little longer to study, and actually learn the material.

•

296. You need to know professors aren't idiots. They're now using tools such as turnitin.com that can spot a plagiarized paragraph copied from a Bulgarian Web site.

•

297. You need to know that if you have your act together, you don't have to cheat. Allow plenty of time, do your paper in stages, work with the writing center—it's that simple.

You Need to Know How to Manage Your Time Since Your Mom Is No Longer Managing It for You

298. You need to know to spend four hours in the library before you spend four hours clubbing. Students who get the order reversed spend the spring semester with their mom.

•

299. You need to know you could easily wind up in classes that meet at 8 a.m., 12 noon, and 4 p.m. What you do in between those classes will determine whether you go to medical school as a student or an experiment.

•

300. You need to know that success in college is based on how well you do things you don't want to do when you don't want to do them.

•

301. You need to know that having a full schedule isn't the same thing as accomplishing something that leads to graduation. Some students have a full schedule of tanning, partying, and studying their boyfriends.

302.   You need to know you'll feel like you don't have enough time to study when the truth is you don't have enough time to party, hold court in the student center, suntan, play tennis, nap, play video games, take two hours for lunch, catch a movie, go to a sorority meeting, spend two hours on Facebook, and *then* study. But you do have time to study.

•

303.   You need to know to invest in a Blackberry or even an old-fashioned pen-and-paper personal day planner. Carry it with you everywhere. Write in it when a professor announces homework or tests. Read tomorrow's plans tonight so you're prepared for . . . well . . . tomorrow.

•

304.   You need to know that students who organize their research and lecture notes using database software tend to do better. Curiously, they tend to run companies later in life as well.

305.   You need to know that being organized has nothing to do with being neat and clean. It simply means being able to find what you're looking for quickly and accomplishing what you want to accomplish efficiently.

•

306.   You need to know that 52 percent of students surveyed felt that partying did not affect their grades. The other 48 percent said partying did affect their grades—and they had a swell time. From what they could remember.

You Need to Know There's More to a Fraternity or Sorority Than Toga Parties (Well, a Little More)

307.   You need to know no one
thinks twice if you're not a Greek.
In fact, a lot of kids are opting out.

•

308.   You need to know rush week can
make perfectly sane people nuts.
Especially girls and moms.

•

309.   You need to know to be yourself.
Acting like somebody you're not will only
confuse everybody. Including you.

•

310.   You need to know the average GPA required
of the fraternity you want to join. If it's around 2.5,
you'll be hanging with a bunch of janitors. If it's
around 3.8, you'll make friends with future CEOs.

•

311.   You need to know that the
Greek system offers great ways to get
involved in campus leadership roles.

312. You need to know whether your fraternity
has ever been written up for underage drinking.
While that sounds fun, it means freshmen have
been taken to the hospital after parties because
they were vomiting their guts up. Not fun.

•

**313. You need to know it's
possible to join a fraternity and
not drink. It's possible.**

•

314. You need to know that it's perfectly
okay to change your mind about joining a frat.
You don't have to stay stuck if you realize
you don't like the people.

•

315. You need to know if there's hazing.
Nothing's crazier than a bunch of
twenty-year-olds running torture sessions.

You Need to Know How to Survive the Parties

316.   You need to know to act like you've lived without a curfew before.

•

317.   You need to know that no one has failed to graduate because of spending too little time partying. In fact, those nerds tend to graduate early.

•

318.   You need to know if you stay drunk all weekend, you can lose as much as 30 percent of what you learned the previous week. No matter how hard you studied. Pass the milk.

•

319.   You need to know to tell yourself there's always going to be another party. There may not, however, be another term paper or semester exam.

320. You need to know parties inevitably break out at night. Get your studying done during the day when all is quiet.

•

321. You need to know at least one sober person at a party in case you need help getting home.

•

322. You need to know you'll have a lot more fun if your homework is done.

•

323. You need to know what the word *moderation* means—and to exercise it.

•

324. You need to know that a study group can take the place of a kegger. Only people bring books, not booze. And as the night goes on, they get smarter, not dumber.

325.   You need to know to use partying as a reward for studying. Not a substitution.

•

326.   You need to know students fail out of party schools all the time.

•

327.   You need to know to not accept a drink from any person you don't know.

•

328.   You need to know the person you're leaving the party with.

•

329.   You need to know to bring enough money for a cab.

You Need to Know
More Than You Already
Think You Know about
Drinking and Drugs

330. You need to know people in college drink the same or more as when they were in high school. If you're getting sauced now, save your tuition money and go straight to rehab.

•

331. You need to know the statement "I was drunk" isn't an excuse.

•

332. You need to know you're not better than the kids who do drugs because all you do is get drunk. Your brain is leaking the same fluid as theirs.

•

333. You need to know drunken crowds are dangerous. Whether you're drunk or not.

334. You need to know that the applications for many graduate programs ask if you've ever been convicted of a crime . . . like, oh, a DWI.

•

335. You need to know once you start missing English Literature because of your drinking, your days are numbered. Cheers.

•

336. You need to know that if you find yourself having to lie about your drinking, then you need to look at the truth.

•

337. You need to know if you wake up in the morning with a strange tattoo, you have a drinking problem.

•

338. You need to know if you need just one little drink to make it through class, you have a drinking problem.

339. You need to know if you're continually promising yourself and your boyfriend you're going to quit, you have a drinking problem.

•

340. You need to know if you're drinking to escape from the pressures of college, you have a drinking problem.

•

341. You need to know if you didn't mean to get drunk, you have a drinking problem.

•

342. You need to know that 40 percent of the academic problems students have today are alcohol-related.

•

343. You need to know you won't be considered weird if you don't drink. You'd be just like 30 percent of today's college students.

•

344. You need to know that learning how to hold your liquor means you've trained your liver to work overtime. Get on the transplant list now.

345. You need to know how to
make one drink last all night.

•

346. You need to know that if you've
forgotten how much you've had to drink, it's
time to stop for the night. And call a cab.

•

347. You need to know that if you have to do a
line to be normal for class, you're not normal.

•

348. You need to know borrowing your
roommate's ADD medicine to stay awake for an
exam can make your heart race, give you a panic
attack, and cause you to freak out during the
exam. "I was stoned" isn't an excuse.

•

349. You need to know that a lot of "brilliant"
students never graduate from college because they
graduated from marijuana to meth and then to
speed, crack, and smack. Many now push
grocery carts downtown.

You Need to Know
about Relationships

350. You need to know there's an intimacy
in just holding hands that a lot of college
students have never experienced.

•

**351. You need to know a person who holds your
hand isn't making a long-term commitment.**

•

352. You need to know the absolute worst reason
to attend a college is because your boyfriend or
girlfriend is there. You've decided in advanced to
limit the number of people you meet.

353. You need to know the odds are
your high-school relationship won't last three
months on campus. If God wants you to be
together in four or five years, it doesn't matter
if one of you goes to the moon. You'll be
back together.

•

354. You need to know everything changes
over time. Including people. And relationships.

•

355. You need to know destructive
relationships can wreak havoc on grades,
friendships, and bank accounts.

•

356. You need to know a major reason students
drop out of college is a relationship gone south.

357.   You need to know a healthy relationship can be good for your grades.

•

358.   You need to know gossip spreads fast in a dorm.

•

359.   You need to know college isn't about finding love. Say it with me: "College is about job opportunities."

•

360.   You need to know "no strings attached" is an urban myth. Sex always comes with strings attached.

•

361.   You need to know pregnancy and a baby will really interfere with graduating.

362. You need to know having a relationship
with a crazy person will only make your
life harder than it already is.

•

363. You need to know that a person who won't
let you hang out with your friends now won't think
any better of them in two or three years.

•

364. You need to know you don't have to spend
every waking moment with the person of your
dreams. Really. Go make other friends.

•

365. You need to know that if you're worried
about another person's drug or alcohol abuse, the
bigger issue is why you're attracted to them.

366.   You need to know that someone who calls you all the time to find out where you are or who you are hanging out with needs therapy. And medication. Change your number.

•

367.   You need to know if a person is continually criticizing you or making fun of you and you stay with them, you're in an abusive relationship.

•

368.   You need to know to flee if a person starts abusing you sexually, emotionally, or physically. You can't make them act differently.

•

369.   You need to know a person who has to be with you all the time is dangerous to be alone with.

370. You need to know that a person who is continually blaming you for her problems has problems. Flee.

•

371. You need to know that jealousy isn't romantic. And it can actually be dangerous.

•

372. You need to know the last thing you want to do is tattoo the name of your sophomore-year boyfriend on your back. It's a hard thing to explain to your junior-year boyfriend.

•

373. You need to know casual sex can turn people into emotional basket cases.

374.   You need to know anyone who texts you at 2 a.m. looking for a hookup isn't worth texting back.

•

375.   You need to know alcohol will only make an abusive relationship worse.

•

376.   You need to know college students who normally carry protection forget to use it when they're drunk.

•

377.   You need to know your friends aren't having more sex than you. Especially the disease-free ones.

•

378.   You need to know that "No" is a complete sentence. After that, it's rape.

You Need to Know How to Take Care of Yourself

379.   You need to know college
is not the place to starve yourself.
Your mind needs nutrition.

•

380.   You need to know you're
feeding your mind whether you're
eating grilled fish or fried Oreos.

•

381.   You need to know that a
meal ticket means yes, you can eat as
much and as often as you want to.
No, you don't want to.

•

382.   You need to know vitamins
don't substitute for food.
You learned this in high school.

383. You need to know drinking alcohol causes you to eat more. Hence the term *fat drunk*.

•

384. You need to know to eat three nutritional meals a day of rational portions. Four if you're staying up late studying.

•

385. You need to know that not everything on a salad bar is healthy.

•

386. You need to know you're not hungry just because your boyfriend broke up with you. You're emotionally distraught.

387.   You need to know to exercise
instead of eating when you feel pressure.
It's weird, but you'll feel better and
you won't gain weight.

•

388.   You need to know sleeping
helps your brain unconsciously process the
information you learned and make connections
that lead to new insights. This doesn't happen
trolling through Facebook all night. This doesn't
happen sleeping in class either.

•

389.   You need to know to not call
home every time you sneeze, cough, wheeze,
or run a fever. Call the infirmary. Every
college has one. And it's cheap.

390.   You need to know to stay
on your parents' health insurance
plan—you just have to stay in school.

•

391.   You need to know if you don't
have health insurance, then buy your own
through the college. Accidents happen.
Really nasty, expensive accidents.

•

392.   You need to know that if
you wash your hands regularly, you can
safely hang with your germ-infested friends
without catching the plague.

You Need to Know If
You've Become Mental

393.   You need to know that if
you're trying to decide between taking a test you
haven't studied for or taking a handful of pills, it's
time to call a counselor. Your college has one.

•

394.   You need to know you've become mental
when any of these are true for you:

You've been feeling sad, irritable, or depressed
for most of every day for weeks, if not months.

Activities or people you used to enjoy
don't seem interesting anymore.

You can't seem to get anything done. Like that
English paper due five weeks ago.

You've stop attending class and feel tired all the time.

You have increased or decreased appetite,
or you've lost or gained weight.

You have terminal insomnia.

You've been unable to get out
of bed for two weeks. Because.

You have difficulty concentrating or making
decisions. Like whether you should get out of
bed—and if you get out of bed, whether
you should take off your pajamas.

Your friends say you're weird now.

You seem to want to slug more people than usual.

You cry a lot, no matter where you are. Like in
Biology 101. You feel bad for the frogs.

You feel hopeless and helpless, as if you're
stuck in a dark hole and can't get out.

You think about death a lot.

You've made a suicide plan.

You're bingeing or starving yourself.

395. You need to know that you're not alone. Eighty percent of college campuses today have noted a significant increase in serious psychological problems, including severe stress, depression, anxiety, and panic attacks.

•

396. You need to know you can't just pull yourself out of clinical depression. You can't study yourself out of it. Or eat your way out of it. Or drink your way out of it. You have to deal with it.

•

397. You need to know that if you mix medication with alcohol, you could easily wind up in a hospital or jail.

•

398. You need to know medication can help with symptoms, but not events or circumstances. That is where you need counseling.

You Need to Know to Not Leave Your Faith at Home

399.   You need to know to let go of your preconceptions about how things will work out. God has a plan too.

•

400.   You need to know it's possible to graduate *summa cum laude* and be accepted into a prestigious medical school and still not find meaning in life.

•

401.   You need to know to not set up an intellectual barrier between you and God.

•

402.   You need to know to attend worship services. Even after partying all night before. Research published in the *New York Times* reveals college students who attend religious services regularly do better than those who don't.

403. You need to know the world
that you are about to enter
is full of religion.

•

404. You need to know to be open
to a real encounter with God.

•

405. You need to know it takes spiritual
strength to face adversity. Going to
church on a regular basis helps.

•

406. You need to know you're not
alone in your beliefs. Religious activities
are offered on campuses more now
than in the last century.

407. You need to know to take your
eyes off yourself and ponder how the majority
of the world lives on $2 a day. The more you ask
how you can help, the less you'll dwell on your
own problems. You may even decide you
don't have any real problems.

•

408. You need to know that,
by your sophomore year, you might
find yourself questioning God.
Don't worry. He can handle it.

•

409. You need to know even
prayer can't overcome the
consequences of not studying.

410. You need to know to pursue
more than a degree. Pursue a purpose.

•

411. You need to know God's purpose
for you is the reason you're alive.

You Need to Know How to Tell the Difference Between a Loser Community College and One That Will Propel You to a Four-Year School

412. A good community college:

Has a focus on liberal arts and science

Means your classes are filled with people
who can add and speak English

Has programs designed to keep motivated
students attending classes together

Has an honors program

Offers a curriculum that crosses disciplines

Has professors who hold advanced degrees

Features transfer agreements with four-year
institutions in-state, guaranteeing you admission
and the transfer of core courses if you've kept up your grades

Has a history of placing students
in top four-year institutions

Can point to community leaders who started there

You Need to Know Transferring Can Make You Feel Like a Freshman All Over Again

413.   You need to know transferring schools is a hassle, and unless it's done for reasons of health, finances, or a substantially better college, it might not be worth it.

•

414.   You need to know there are programs—like transition workshops, career-planning workshops, or university experience courses—designed to help transfer students adjust.

•

415.   You need to know to join a group of some kind during your first week of classes. Even if you're not a freshman.

416. You need to know that a lot of the credits you killed yourself to earn at your old school may not transfer to your new one. This is what leads to six-year degree plans.

•

417. You need to know the introductory classes you took at your old school may not have prepared you for the advanced classes at your new one. If so, swallow your pride and take the intro classes again.

•

418. You need to know that if you transferred because you're involved with a person at your new campus, you'll probably transfer again.

You Need to Know
What Cool Things
Could Convince You to
Stay in School

419.   You need to know that
note-taking strategies are available
at the college's tutoring center.

•

420.   You need to know that football,
basketball, and soccer games are where you can
scream, get crazy, and look no dumber than the
forty-year-old in the next section. And your
student ID will get you in cheap.

•

421.   You need to know that networking your
butt off could lead you to meeting, say, the guy
in charge of sports programming for one of the
major networks. Or the woman in charge of PR for
a major Hollywood studio. Happens every day.

422. You need to know to take
advantage of all the incredible things
on campus you have already paid for: movie
nights, plays, guest speakers, museums, concerts,
newspapers, and sometimes cheap massages.

•

423. You need to know to take some
classes that have nothing to do with your core
or major: photography, creative writing, TV
production. Such a class could change
your entire attitude toward college.

•

424. You need to know you could be
a DJ at your campus radio station.

425. You need to know to sneak into a lecture on ethnomusicology or religion or Middle East studies or video production and see what you think.

•

426. You need to know to take archery or golf. Get credit for learning to correct your slice.

•

427. You need to know there's an intramural sports team for the good, the bad, and the ugly.

You Need to Know
How to Keep Money
Problems from Causing
You to Drop Out

428. You need to know the total cost of a four-year school ranges between $100,000 and $200,000. This is why your dad and mom always seem to be in a bad mood.

•

429. You need to know that if you work more than twenty hours a week, you're at a higher risk of dropping out.

•

430. You need to know to not use lack of money as an excuse for leaving school. Money is available to people who will do the work.

431.   You need to know to create and
live by a budget. You need to know
why you're always overdrawn.

•

432.   You need to know you can stil
have a fun social life on a small budget.

•

433.   You need to know that
borrowing money to go to college
is the very best financial decision you
can make at this age. If you graduate.

•

434.   You need to know to check with your
financial aid officer every year to see if
you can turn your loan into a grant.

435. You need to know buying textbooks
at your college bookstore can cost between
$700 and $1000. But you can save a
fortune with just a little effort.

•

436. You need to know to start at
www.bookfinder.com or www.andybrain.com/
archive/textbooks-online.htm.

•

437. You need to know that waiting until classes
start to buy your books won't give you time to shop
the best deals. Many colleges and professors list the
required textbooks on their Web site.

438.   You need to know that many expensive textbooks have a paperback equivalent costing up to 90 percent less than the hardcover edition. Check with your professor and then head to the Web.

•

439.   You need to know to use your student loan money to actually finance your education. Not a spiffy new BMW.

•

440.   You need to know to fill out the FAFSA even if your parents are heart surgeons. All money starts here.

441. You need to know college
tuition aid also comes in the form of loans.
With really favorable interest rates.
And they're available regardless of need.

•

**442. You need to know to live within
your means, as meager as they are.**

•

443. You need to know to not trade
in the paid-for car your parents gave
you for a new leased one. Then
you'd have car payments.

444. You need to know that campus jobs pay less, but give you greater scheduling flexibility. That, plus low transportation expenses, makes it a pretty good trade.

•

445. You need to know that one of the best things about a campus job is you wind up sitting on your butt most of the day. In other words, they'll pay you to study. Sweet.

•

446. You need to know to not let a debilitating injury to you or your parents derail your college plans. Visit your financial aid office and explain what happened. Things can be worked out.

447. You need to know
homework is much easier to finish
if you don't have to work two jobs
to meet credit card payments.

•

448. You need to know how to evaluate
credit card offers with all their different interest
rates and annual fees. This is a seventh-grade math
skill that many college freshmen don't have.

•

449. You need to know credit card debt
is a major reason kids drop out of college.

450.   You need to know, since
you're the legal age to sign up for a
credit card, you're also the legal age
to be sued for nonpayment.

•

451.   You need to know a credit
card doesn't make you independent.
Money makes you independent.

•

452.   You need to know a manageable
$30-a-month credit card payment can skyrocket
up to $300 a month if you are late on one payment
and if you go over your credit limit.

453. You need to know outstanding credit card debt can cost you housing, graduate school admission, your car, a job, maybe even your ability to secure school loans.

•

454. You need to know to not lend your car. An unfortunate wreck, cancelled insurance, and lawsuits can end the brightest college career.

•

455. You need to know to maintain solid financial status. Overdraft charges and fees for bounced checks or late payments can reduce you to living on bean dip.

456. You need to know to avoid
cash-advance stores. Interest begins accruing the
day you walk in. And the Mob charges less.

•

457. You need to know that when you live on
campus, you don't have utility bills. If you live off
campus, utility bills are those things you've been
throwing away thinking they're junk mail.

•

458. You need to know you can sell
your blood only a few times a year.

•

459. You need to know to start
clipping coupons if you're living in an
apartment. Especially on Sunday.
They can slash your grocery bill.

You Need to Know How to Handle Your Parents

460.   You need to know your parents
will eventually get over your leaving
home. So if your mother cries whenever
you call, be patient with her.

•

461.   You need to know you still
need your parents' advice and support.
Don't leave home without it.

•

462.   You need to know to send
them a letter every now and then.
With a stamp. And not asking for money.

463. You need to know your parents
are making sacrifices so you can go to college.
Don't be flippant about the money.

•

464. You need to know that if Mom and
Dad are paying for college, they will continually
bug you about your grades.

•

465. You need to know they won't send
you money every time you call.

•

466. You need to know you might actually
have better conversations with your parents
now that you don't see them every day.

467. You need to know to show your parents your report card. If you're afraid to, use that as a wake-up call.

•

468. You need to know that while it's your parents' money, it's your life. You have to decide what field interests you, what school you want to attend, or if you want to take a semester off.

•

469. You need to know you can still go on a trip with your parents even though you're in college. It just might do all of you good.

You Need to Know
It's Time to Think
Like an Adult

470. You need to know it's normal
to miss Mom's cooking and to not want to be
responsible for anything. It's also normal
to like, you know, get over it.

•

471. You need to know that in college
you will acquire behaviors that will last into
adulthood. And this includes drinking, thinking,
organization, responsibility, how you
treat the opposite sex—everything.

•

472. You need to know just
because you *can* do something
doesn't mean you *should*.

473. You need to know that if you're "above average," you can shave a year off college by taking between eighteen and twenty-one units a semester. This means less partying, but you could start making money that much sooner.

•

474. You need to know the best cure for worrying in bed is getting up and studying.

•

475. You need to know why you failed a test. And make the necessary changes to pass the next one.

476. You need to know that blowing
a course or two isn't the end of the world. People
have recovered from a bad semester
to go on to medical school.

•

477. You need to know to not go around thinking
your professors hate you if you're failing.

•

478. You need to know to not
take pictures of your body parts with
your camera phone and then send them
out to your address book. This usually
results in total humiliation.

•

479. You need to know that knowing
too few people causes just as many
problems as having too much fun.

480. You need to know different people flower at different times. It could happen to you during your sophomore year. Or when you're forty.

•

481. You need to know that if you're feeling like everyone is talking about you, you've seriously underestimated other college students' tendency to think only about themselves.

•

482. You need to know that developing the ability to cope with adversity is a rite of passage into adulthood.

483. You need to know the solution to having a difficult time is rarely dropping out of school. But it may be dropping a difficult course. And picking it up in the summer.

•

484. You need to know that if you need your parents to run interference for you in college, your tuition is probably a waste of money.

•

485. You need to know that one day you'll be twenty-two. If you work hard enough, you can be a twenty-two-year-old college graduate. Or else you could be a twenty-two-year-old dropout.

486. You need to know to memorize
your Social Security number.
You'll be asked for it a lot.

•

487. You need to know someone has to
clean the dorm, change the sheets, and
pay the bills. And Mom's at home.

•

488. You need to know a life
spent in the pursuit of happiness
results in anything but.

•

489. You need to know winning isn't the
only thing in life. People who think that
start cutting corners early.

490. You need to know that vacationing in Cabo
instead of working as a summer intern will come
back to haunt you when all the graduates who
interned have jobs and you have a deep, dark tan.

•

491. You need to know a high IQ doesn't
determine wealth. Education, ambition,
hard work, and grace play huge roles. People
with average IQs get rich all the time.

•

492. You need to know many employers view
your GPA as the best indicator of work success.

•

493. You need to know many companies
don't want to interview anyone with
less than a 3.0 grade point.

494. You need to know working your way through college isn't fun—especially when you're burning your hands in some fast-food kitchen while other students are partying their drunken heads off. But you're prioritizing, showing responsibility, and practicing good decision making—all transferable job skills. And what could possibly show up on the Internet?

•

495. You need to know you're not a smarter, wiser, or infinitely more capable human being than your parents. Otherwise you wouldn't be calling home for money.

•

496. You need to know when you're failing—and get some help. Don't lie to yourself until the end of the semester.

497. You need to know that if you
quit school, the odds are you won't come
back at all. And the longer you're out,
the worse the odds become.

•

498. You need to know it's smarter to change your
major now than to one day find yourself
stuck in a career you hate.

•

499. You need to know you control
the issues that determine your success.

•

500. You need to know you'll probably
grow apart from some of your close
high-school friends. Especially the ones who
continue to act like they're in high school.

501. You need to know the Top 10 Qualities Employers Seek in Job Candidates

(or Things You Should Have Learned in Four Years):

1. Communication skills

2. Motivation/Initiative

3. Teamwork

4. Leadership

5. Academic Achievement/GPA

6. Interpersonal skills

7. Flexibility/Adaptability

8. Technical Skills

9. Honesty and Integrity

10. Analytical/Problem-Solving Skills

You Need to Know
Life Is Difficult So You
Won't Get Discouraged
and Move Home

502. You need to know
adulthood is not for sissies.

•

503. You need to know you
now pay the bills.

•

504. You need to know everybody isn't
doing better than you are. In fact, most
of the world isn't doing as well as you are.

•

505. You need to know the media is selling
you on a lifestyle that is essentially unobtainable.

•

506. You need to know things are
rarely as good or as bad as they seem.

507. You need to know the cure for
sitting around feeling miserable and depressed
is to go outside and find somebody to serve.

•

508. You need to know young adulthood
means apartments are smaller, clothes are
cheaper, money is tighter, and public
transportation could be involved.

•

509. You need to know the
solution to running low on money
isn't to start spending more.

•

510. You need to know the world
is filled with unreasonable people.
And you may work for one of them.

511. You need to know the difference between owning a Mercedes or washing it for a living, is education.

•

512. You need to know "overnight successes" have often toiled twenty years to become one.

•

513. You need to know to seek the advice of a mentor. Not the wisdom of your unemployed club friends.

•

514. You need to know your parents aren't rich. They just have more money now that their kids are out of the house.

•

515. You need to know everybody struggles. Even trust-fund babies.

516. You need to know that
nobody wants to hear you whine.

•

517. You need to know everybody
has days when the toilets back up.
God isn't picking on you.

•

518. You need to know that contrary to popular
belief, the amount of money people spend isn't
indicative of their wealth, but their values.

•

519. You need to know you've worked all
your life to get to exactly where you are now.
Even if you're just sleeping on the couch.

520. You need to know Bill Gates lost
$40 billion in eighteen months, Donald Trump
declared bankruptcy, and Michael Jordan couldn't
make his high-school basketball team.

•

521. You need to know if
getting a good job were so easy,
everybody would have one.

•

522. You need to know that when
comparing yourself to anyone else,
you're comparing God's handiwork.

•

523. You need to know overcoming difficult
times is how people gain self-respect.
And the respect of others.

524. You need to know to not
lose your belief in miracles.

•

525. You need to know the secret to solving
paralyzing problems isn't to take to
the couch, but to start taking action.

•

526. You need to know life's
challenges make us stronger, better,
healthier, more spiritual, and more grateful
human beings. After we freak out.

•

527. You need to know that in five years you don't
have to be the same person you are today. You
could have earned a law degree, fed the hungry in
Africa, or defended your country.

528.   You need to know
victims are never happy.

•

529.   You need to know to not
wait until there are helicopters
circling overhead to start a prayer life.

•

530.   You need to know that if you
get laid off, it doesn't mean you'll spend
the rest of your life in a Chevrolet.
It just means God has other plans.

•

531.   You need to know the
biggest difference between childhood
and adulthood is that in adulthood,
you really can't give up.

532. You need to know you'll feel
a lot better about everything if you get
a good night's sleep. Exhaustion can
make everything seem darker.

•

533. You need to know growing up
takes moving out. And moving on.

You Need to Know How
to Not Look Stupid
Because People Will
Notice and You'll
Have to Move Home

534.   You need to know truly
independent people don't scream they're
independent with their hand held out.

•

535.   You need to know how to type without
looking at the keyboard. Or be prepared for a
minimum-wage job with hazardous-duty pay.

•

536.   You need to know many
companies would prefer not to
see your tattoos. Or nose ring.

•

537.   You need to know your role
models shouldn't be each other.

538. You need to know
Hollywood isn't hiring.

•

539. You need to know the successful
person does things other people don't
like to do. Like get organized.

•

540. You need to know that if you
sleep around, it will get around.

•

541. You need to know to keep up
with what's going on in the world.

•

542. You should consider that
yes, as impossible as it may seem,
you could be wrong.

543. You need to know one of
the best tools for not looking dumb
is to ask questions of people.

•

544. You need to know it's impossible
to learn anything while talking.

•

545. You need to know to refrain from sending
any e-mail written in the heat of the moment. In
certain circumstances, it could be called evidence.

•

546. You need to know to not
naively believe everyone is good and
has your best interest at heart.

547. You need to know to never
believe e-mails saying you just won a
contest in Belgium you never entered.

•

548. You need to know to not
announce you're seeking answers from
a tarot card reader. People will assume
you're part of the lunatic fringe.

•

549. You need to know how to listen
without tuning out 50 percent.

•

550. You need to know spell-check can help
you look smarter. Careers are derailed over poor
writing and spelling.

551. You need to know "Whatever" isn't a
sentence. It's evidence of a fragile mind.

•

552. You need to know that
if you don't know what you're
talking about, stay silent.

•

553. You need to know to not
believe everything you hear.

554. You need to know that
one of the signs of a loser is to never
plan ahead. Going with the flow usually
means going down the drain.

•

555. You need to know that
boasting makes people wonder
what's really wrong with you.

•

556. You need to know how to carry on a
conversation without using profanity.

•

557. You need to know to
follow instructions. Houses are
set on fire over this.

558. You need to know how to defend a position without yelling, swearing, or door slamming. And it's a bonus if you know what you're talking about.

•

559. You need to know alcohol causes bad breath. You should also know that while you can't smell it, everybody else can.

•

560. You need to know to write notes to yourself. The alternative is to rely on a memory that can't remember to call your mother.

•

561. You need to know telling the truth drastically limits one's chances of being humiliated, fired, or sued.

562.   You need to know good manners
so stun people that favors, promotions,
and recommendations follow.

•

563.   You need to know that having three or four
drinks doesn't make you sound any smarter. Unless
you're talking to a person who's had five.

•

564.   You need to know the fine
art of small talk. It beats standing
alone with a potted plant all night when
you could be chatting up the most
important person in the room.

565. You need to know to read the
Bible before you argue about it.

•

566. You need to know to not confuse
fiction with nonfiction books and movies.
It's the latest rage today.

You Need to Know
How to Get a Job So
You Can Make Your Own
Money and Not Have
to Move Home

567.   You need to know what you're
capable of doing for a living. Not
just what you'd like to do.

•

568.   You need to know the best time
to start networking is way before you
actually need a network. Or else
you're just hitting up strangers for jobs.

•

569.   You need to know employers
care more about a college degree than
where the diploma is from. Most CEOs
of the biggest corporations didn't
go to prestigious schools.

•

570.   You need to know your chances of
becoming among the biggest earners in any
profession—like acting—are extremely small.

571.   You need to know that finding
a job is, in itself, a full-time job. With
weekend and evening work involved.

•

572.   You need to know your
résumé has fifteen seconds to get
the attention of an HR director.

•

573.   You need to know that if you wait
until you graduate from college to pump up
your résumé, you've waited too long.

•

574.   You need to know building a résumé
doesn't mean lying or exaggerating. It
means accomplishing.

•

575.   You need to know to Google
your name. See what pops up.
Prospective employers will.

576. You need to know your cover
letter is the door opener. Or door closer.

•

577. You need to know there are a
plethora of books, software, and services to
help you create a résumé and a cover letter.
And your competition is using them.

•

578. You need to know to never
start a cover letter with "Dear Sir or Madam."
It says you were too unmotivated to
learn the interviewer's name.

•

579. You need to know to apply for a specific
position. Saying, "I'll do anything" on your résumé
will cause it to mysteriously disappear.

580. You need to know the people you meet in
college and graduate schools are future clients,
customers, or employers. Don't lose track of them.

•

581. You need to know employers will
be checking your MySpace or Facebook pages.
What your friends find hilarious will
usually result in rejection letters.

•

582. You need to know the difference
between networking and hanging in
bars late at night with a bunch of out-of-work
goobers talking about getting a job.

•

583. You need to know to never, ever
bad-mouth another company or person
in an interview. Kiss of death.

584. You need to know to arrive early
to each interview, if for no other reason
than to avoid a speeding ticket.

•

585. You need to know to not dress like a
model or rock star unless
you're interviewing to be one.

•

586. You should ask God to
walk into the interview with you.

You need to know to plan and practice
your answers to the following questions:

•

587. *"Tell me about yourself."* You need to
be able to get to the point about your goals,
experience, interests, and communication skills.

•

588. *"What are your strengths?"* This is the
key time to point out your characteristics
that make you perfect for the job.

•

589. *"What are your weaknesses?"*
You need to know that saying, "I work
too hard" or "I'm a perfectionist"
makes interviewers gag. Just point
out your obvious inexperience
as the greatest weakness.

590. *"Why do you want to work here?"*
This is where Internet research pays off. You
should say, "I've always wanted to work for a
company that does things the way you do . . ."
and talk about what you've learned.

•

591. *"Why should we hire you?"*
This is a good time to mention the
word *desire* as well as talk about your
unique strengths and experiences that
make you ideal for the job.

•

592. *"What would you do in a particular situation*?"
This is a trick question. You should ask the
interviewer, "What's my goal?" before responding.

593. You need to know to ask how your
performance will be measured, will
you be transferred, and how are
top employees rewarded.

•

594. You should ask questions other prospects
might not: "Is management stable? What about
training programs? Will the company fund
additional education?"

•

595. You need to know to not give out salary
information until you receive an offer. And this
could take two or three interviews.

596.   You need to know a thank-you
note will make you look more professional
than the last ten goobers who walked
in the door, and you can add
anything you forgot to say.

•

597.   You need to know to interview
with the person who will be your actual boss.
This prevents any surprises down the road.

•

598.   You should ask what happened to
the person who had the job before you.
Were they promoted? Fired? Transferred?
Eloped with the boss? You need to know.

599.   You need to remember the greater goal in negotiations is not to get fifty grand a year. It's to get hired, get trained, get experience, build your value, get money, and get out of the house.

•

600.   You need to know not to hold out for the "perfect" job. You have forty or fifty years to find that.

•

601.   You need to know to celebrate your job offer. It's a very cool thing.

•

602.   You need to know to take the health insurance offered, even though it reduces your paycheck. A $10,000-a-day hospitalization will really ruin party plans.

You Need to Know How
to Keep a Job and Get
Promoted So You Don't
Get Fired and Have to
Move Home

603. You need to know that beginning right now you're in an intense, high-stakes competition for a life unimaginable by most of the planet.

•

604. You need to know that college didn't teach you half the stuff you need to know about your job.

•

605. You need to know to be more concerned with showing up on time than taking time off.

•

606. You need to know to raise your hand when you're confused or sinking under water. Don't wait till the exit interview.

607. You need to know the keys to promotion are ambition, creativity, and the ability to grow on the job.

•

608. You need to know the world beyond your friends cares little that you have a Rolex or Mercedes. The world cares about results.

•

609. You need to know that if you don't spread office gossip, you'll never have to apologize to anybody.

•

610. You need to know to prepare for meetings and presentations. The alternatives are hot flashes, hiccups, and looking stupid.

611. You need to know co-workers who don't like you can derail career plans. Think teamwork.

•

612. You need to know to never use the words *not my job* if you're making long-term career plans.

•

613. You need to know to congratulate your co-workers for jobs well done. Even if you hate their guts and feel like management likes them better.

•

614. You need to know the first year on the job impacts your long-term advancement, salary, satisfaction, and career track.

615.   You should remember nobody
likes ideas from people who don't know what
they're talking about. Especially newly hired
graduates who think they know everything.

•

616.   You need to know the only people
allowed to be prima donnas are the bosses and
the people who bring in the most business.

•

617.   You need to know to stay alert
in meetings. Yawning and napping
should have ended in English Lit.

•

618.   You should understand that every business,
even a dentist's office, is about politics.

619. You need to know to say
"thank you" to co-workers regularly.
It breeds enormous goodwill.

•

**620. You need to know to
learn the janitor's name.**

•

621. You need to know that taking office
supplies, making personal long-distance
calls on the company phone, and
padding expenses is stealing.

•

**622. You need to know to
read the company manual.**

•

623. You need to know to not criticize anything
the first six months. You could be stomping
on the president's idea and not realize it.

624.   You need to know that
not everything you do will generate
praise. Even if it's well done.

•

625.   You need to know jerks
sometimes have a way of getting
promoted. It happens.

•

626.   You need to know to bring
your boss a solution every time
you bring up a problem.

•

627.   You need to know how to figure things out
on your own. Most of the world's secrets can be
unlocked with Google, determination, and coffee.

•

628.   You need to remember
excuses don't lead to promotions.

629. You need to know helping out fellow employees is a proven way to build goodwill.

•

630. You need to know that making yourself irreplaceable to your clients and bosses is a secret to raises and promotions.

•

631. You need to know that if you dress provocatively on the job, everyone will notice: clients, bosses, bosses' wives. Human Resources.

•

632. You need to know you have a choice: partying all night or functioning effectively in the business world the next morning.

633. You need to know how to discern unspoken, on-the-job expectations.

•

634. You need to know that whining about not being promoted will get you labeled a malcontent.

•

635. You need to know to find a mentor at the office who can champion your cause. This is how careers are launched.

•

636. You need to know to ask for more responsibility before you ask for a raise.

•

637. You need to know that no one gets promoted six months into a job. But a lot of people get promoted because the person above them impatiently quits.

638. You need to know to keep your thoughts about the company you work for to yourself. And off the Internet.

•

639. You need to know you'll get more notice for working late than you will for coming in early.

•

640. You need to know it often takes longer than eight-to-five to get the job done.

•

641. You need to know it's poisonous to compare salaries with anyone else in the office.

642. You need to know to make a list every night of what you need to accomplish the next day. Knowing what to do is how things get done.

•

643. You need to know to be careful with office romances. And more careful with office romance breakups.

•

644. You need to know that if you do your job well, you are entitled to raises and promotions. And often these have to be negotiated.

•

645. You need to know there's nothing disloyal about interviewing with other companies. It's how people get raises faster.

646. You need to know a great negotiation ploy in discussing raises is talking about another job offer. It's even more effective if you have one.

•

647. You need to know that if you've done your work well but others are getting raises and promotions, it's time to go.

•

648. You need to know to take several things into consideration besides money when deciding on another job. Like opportunity, benefits, and travel.

•

649. You need to know to not be afraid of changing jobs. Be afraid of losing your passion.

650.   You need to know to not resign
until you've accepted another offer
in writing. Until then, it's all rumor.

•

651.   You need to know to resign the
right way: personally, to your boss, and
without bad-mouthing anybody.

•

652.   You need to know one of life's most
baffling mysteries is how people come in and
out of one's life. Don't burn any bridges.

•

653.   You need to remember the
first job is just that.

You Need to Know How to
Live on a Starting Salary
So You Won't Go Broke
and Have to Move Home

654. You need to know that life, unlike college, doesn't come with a meal card. Budgeting is in order.

•

655. You need to know you can save a fortune by cooking. Your kitchen isn't there to just store beer.

•

656. You need to know to pay off your fines and rejoin the library. It's a way to save a fortune in book and movie rental costs.

•

657. You need to know public transportation is cheaper than expensive gasoline and parking meters.

658.   You need to know the prices in supermarkets are two to three times less than in convenience stores. Of course, it may require shopping at an hour other than 3 a.m.

•

659.   You need to know about resale stores. The bargains on quality, barely used clothes are amazing.

•

660.   You need to know to not jump into the real estate market with an adjustable rate mortgage. A $900-a-month payment can balloon to an $1800-a month payment and foreclosure in the blink of an eye.

•

661.   You need to know you won't start out on your own living at the standard your parents provided. For many, this is a news flash.

662. You need to know that if you are afraid to
open the bills, it's time to stop spending.

•

663. You need to know to never take an instant
tax refund from anybody. The fee is a whopping 20
percent. And the government isn't *that* slow.

•

664. You need to know to never,
ever take a cash advance from one credit
card to make a payment on another.
This is the way losers live.

•

665. You need to know having roommates
saves big money. Just about everyone
can learn to be agreeable.

666. You need to know that
basing your happiness on how you compare
financially to your friends is a sure ticket to misery.

•

667. You need to know that making a budget
won't only help you live within your means now,
but give you a road map for wealth down the road.

•

668. You need to know to call a
credit counseling service if your
bills are out of hand.

•

669. You need to know that one
big secret to stretching money is
living near one's work.

670.   You need to know the difference between a want and a need before you spend your money. For instance, you need a car that runs, not a new Beamer.

•

671.   You need to know to save something every month. Call it an emergency fund so you don't have to move home.

•

672.   You need to know to always deposit your paycheck in a bank, and to never cash it at a check-cashing store. You may as well be dealing with the Mob since you'll be paying Mob rates.

•

673.   You need to know customers of "payday" loan companies often pay up to 1000 percent of their loan value. This insures the poor will remain poor.

674. You need to know sometimes
life takes working two jobs.

•

675. You need to know low automobile
insurance rates depend as much on your
credit as your driving record.

•

676. You need to know that delayed gratification
will help you avoid a majority of financial issues.

•

677. You need to know that if you spend all your
money on nightclubs and impressing people, you'll
quickly have an impressive amount of debt.

•

678. You need to know that if you can't
afford to pay cash, you can't afford it.

679. You need to know using a
credit card is, in reality, taking out a
short-term, very high-interest loan.

•

680. You need to know credit cards cause
you to spend future income on present-day
wants. The solution is to want less.

•

681. You need to know if you're one day late
paying on a 0-percent-interest credit card, the interest
could zoom to a breathtaking 18 percent. That doesn't
just bite, it bites and sucks and is impossible to pay
off with minimum monthly payments.

•

682. You need to know that unless you
pay twice the minimum monthly payment,
credit card balances never really go away.

683.   You need to know the easiest
way to gain control of your finances is to track
your spending. Then you can make decisions
on what to live without: Imported beer?
Tanning salon? Designer shoes?

•

684.   You need to know credit
union rates are usually better than the
bank for borrowing and saving. Banks
would prefer you not know this.

•

685.   You need to know balancing
your account every month saves nasty
surprises and overdraft charges—
and involves sixth-grade math skills.

686.   You need to know a debt collector can't say, "We'll take your house," or "We'll tell your boss," or "We'll tell your parents." And they can't demand payment that day.

•

687.   You need to know that one of the keys to good credit is continually monitoring your credit report. And raising heck when it's wrong.

•

688.   You need to know banks aren't doing anybody any favors by making loans. So comparison-shop even the good offers.

689. You need to know that using a credit card to pile up travel awards works only if the credit card is paid in full every month. Failure to do so means really expensive "free" airline tickets.

•

690. You need to know that college loans can be consolidated, payment plans can be changed, and sometimes loans can be deferred. Just don't let payments pile up.

•

691. You need to know there are interest-rate calculators all over the Internet to help you calculate the true cost of MasterCarding a $1000 TV. (In some cases it can be up to five figures.)

692. You need to know a credit
card company will often lower the interest
rate of any customer in good standing who
demands it. Just ask for a supervisor.

•

693. You need to know you if you
forget to take your ATM receipt, you
could likely find your banking information
posted on the Internet.

•

694. You need to know one of the proven
keys to prosperity is giving back to God
even when there's not a lot to start with.

You Need to Know How to Locate and Conduct Yourself in Your First Apartment So You're Not Thrown Out and Have to Move Home

695. You need to know to tell even the mail carrier you're looking for an apartment. You never know whose cousin's brother's aunt has a place.

•

696. You need to know to not leave home without renters' insurance. You're betting against the house without it. Literally.

•

697. You need to know it's not your parent's name going on the lease contract. And you can't just decide you don't like the small closets after three months and split.

•

698. You need to know to read and understand your lease. Don't sign and wonder.

699. You need to know that if more
than a third of your salary goes to rent,
you will miss out on a lot of life.

•

700. You need to know to Google the
address of any place you're thinking about
renting. See what headlines come up.

•

701. You need to know that unless
you find an apartment with utilities included,
you'll have to learn to turn off the lights
and turn down thermostats.

•

702. You need to know to put off that
plasma TV purchase until after you move in.
Some leases require the renter to have
a healthy savings account.

703. You need to know apartments pull credit ratings. Anything under 620 essentially tells the management they're staring at a deadbeat.

•

704. You need to know to visit with a couple of tenants to see how they like the place, if the management is responsive, and if the dudes upstairs dance all night.

•

705. You need to know to not be so in love with the look of a place, you fail to ask about parking, pets, on-site management, maintenance, and laundry rooms. These are the things that will drive you nuts.

706.   You need to know to make sure
everything works before you sign: lights, toilet,
oven, air conditioner, heater, stove,
and showers. After you sign, management
may not be responsible for repairs.

•

707.   You need to know to send change-of-address
information to everybody you owe money
to or who might send you money.

•

708.   You need to know to take
pictures of anything broken or torn or
scraped the day you move in. Doing it six
months later will be unconvincing
proof and may lead to loss of deposit.

709.   You need to know what happens
if you break the lease. It usually goes
under the title "Not Advisable."

•

710.   You need to know to not pay
a dime to anyone until the lease is signed.
You have the power of the pen.

•

711.   You need to know stupid
roommates are expensive. There's property
damage, unpaid rent, and accumulated fines you
could find yourself responsible for.

•

712.   You need to know to disinfect every
surface of the entire apartment the day you move
in. And to not stop until your mother will
touch things without rubber gloves.

713. You need to know that the big, dark, ugly thing running around the silverware drawer is a roach, and he has thousands of drinking buddies. The National Guard would be of no help now.

•

714. You need to know that living with a friend or a lover just might kill the whole relationship.

•

715. You need to know that all apartments and condos have rules. And failure to follow those rules could mean getting tossed out on the street without a deposit refund.

716. You need to know to give your elderly neighbors fair warning you are having people over who could be dancing and screaming at the top of their lungs. Ask them to call you before they call the law.

•

717. You need to know to not keep any bicycle you want to see again chained to a bike rack outside. Its days are numbered.

•

718. You need to know you can furnish your apartment for a song at www.craigslist.com.

•

719. You need to know to be proud of your place. You're now home.

You Need to Know Even More about Relationships So a Bad One Won't Force You to Move Home

720.   You need to know failed relationships are one
of the main reasons adult kids move home.

•

721.   You need to know to marry for character.

•

722.   You need to know to not worry
about being alone. God has plans.

•

723.   You need to know being alone is a good
way to get to know yourself. (And if you don't like
who you are, a relationship is doomed.)

•

724.   You need to know to stay
away from emotionally unavailable
people who are afraid of commitment.
Marriage won't make them any more available.

725.   You need to know that following someone, driving past their house, and posting things about them on the Internet indicates a need for therapy.

•

726.   You need to know, when looking up prospects on the Internet, that just because someone says they're a single doctor doesn't mean they're not really a married chicken separator with eight kids.

•

727.   You need to know that if you can't invite God into the bedroom, then it's no place for you either.

•

728.   You need to know some people would rather work fifteen hours a day than go home to a person who loves them. And marrying them doesn't change them.

729. You need to know when you break
up with somebody, not to continue to
hang out with that person. Find new friends.

•

730. You need to know that seeking perfection
in a mate will assure you of a lifetime of
loneliness and disappointment.

•

731. You need to know to never miss
an opportunity to tell someone
how important they are to you.

•

732. You need to know you're
no picnic to live with either.

•

733. You need to know words can tear
at a relationship as fast as actions.

734. You need to know there's no biblical reason to wait for the other person to apologize first.

•

735. You need to know to not spend more time on your wedding than on strengthening your relationship. A lot of couples get it wrong here.

•

736. You need to know if you are constantly walking on eggshells around another person, it's time to put on a pair of fast running shoes. And flee.

•

737. You need to know to not play house. Relationships should be kept sacred.

738.   You need to know sex produces babies. A lot of people forget this in the heat of the moment.

•

739.   You need to know birth control devices aren't as easy to use as you think. Some even require practice.

•

740.   You need to know the Pill can add to the risk of heart disease, high blood pressure, and blood clots. It can also cause nausea and increased appetite.

•

741.   You need to know most single parents are mothers.

•

742.   You need to know that half of the unmarried women who give birth live below the poverty line.

743. You need to know an abortion will haunt both parents for the rest of your lives.

•

744. You need to know that many of the longest-lasting marriages have started with the smallest of weddings.

•

745. You need to know that when compassion, forgiveness, kindness, and gentleness leave a relationship, love is not too far behind.

•

746. You need to know that if a person breaks your heart time and again, it will happen again.

•

747. You need to know to graduate from college before you get married.

748. You need to know counseling for couples is a way to make sure everyone is grown-up enough to get married. A lot of churches offer this.

•

749. You need to know the number one cause of divorce is finances.

•

750. You need to know having kids does nothing to make a couple's finances better.

•

751. You need to know you can't change somebody by marrying them. Once screwy, always screwy.

•

752. You should learn the art of seeing the other point of view.

753.   You need to know old high-school friends are rarely welcome in an adult relationship.

•

754.   You need to know to start saving for retirement the day after your honeymoon.

•

755.   You need to know the little everyday criticisms, bullying, and broken promises are what turn a marriage toward the road to Antarctica.

•

756.   You need to know that if you're in a failing relationship, you're not the victim. You're half the problem.

•

757.   You need to know that a strong marriage requires two strong people.

758.   You need to know that people curiously
need to hear the words "I love you"
a lot. Even after the wedding.

•

759.   You need to know that fear
poisons a marriage. And people get
afraid when they feel powerless.

•

760.   You need to know you can either
be happy or you can be right. People who
are right all the time are single.

•

761.   You need to know the most intimate act a
couple can do together is pray together.

•

762.   You need to know that once you get married,
God has an interest in seeing you stay married.

763. You need to know that trust is one of those curious things that, when lost, is hard to find again.

•

764. You need to know if you feel a need to control someone else's mood, degree of happiness, amount of drinking, or level of fear, what you really need is a good 12-step program.

•

765. You need to know that there is no excuse for abuse in a relationship.

•

766. You need to know that no relationship should force you to compromise your principles or self-respect.

•

767. You need to know making a budget is one of the most important things a couple can do. Before marriage.

768. You need to know if you're fighting about money, you need to start talking about it.

•

769. You need to know to pay bills together. It holds the fear down.

•

770. You need to know to not confuse emotional intimacy with sexual intimacy. Sex has nothing to do with feeling respected, admired, worthy, and loved.

•

771. You need to know the hardest part about saving a troubled marriage is recognizing and acknowledging it's in trouble in the first place.

•

772. You need to know if people don't find emotional intimacy in a relationship, they might look for it someplace else.

773.   You need to know prayer strengthens a relationship. But prayer without action is nothing.

●

774.   You need to know a marriage
is like a bank account: you're either making
deposits or taking withdrawals.

●

775.   You need to know that after the
"bloom" wears off, love is a decision.

●

776. You need to know to stay and work it out.

You Need to Know How to Live without Mom Waking You Up, Doing Your Laundry, and Taking Care of You, or Else You'll Move Home

777.   You need to know vacuuming doesn't wear
out a carpet. Dirt and grime wear out a carpet.
Vacuuming actually makes it last longer.

•

778.   You need to know that mold and mildew are
evidence your place is becoming a toxic dump.

•

779.   You need to know that roaches and
ants are usually invited in by food lying
around on the floor and counters.

•

780.   You need to know the great
thing about the dishwasher is that it can
be used to clean toothbrushes, oven vents,
knobs, hairbrushes, trays—anything that's
bacteria-laden, gross, and fits inside.

781. You need to know to use doormats.
A pound of dirt is often found there.

•

782. You need to know human
hair wreaks havoc on drains.

•

783. You should learn to put everything
back in the refrigerator. And not eat
anything that's been lying out for three days.

•

784. You should know a dirty
apartment can make you sick.

•

785. You need to know to buy a loud,
obnoxious alarm clock with a snooze
button. You have to get up at 6 a.m. now.

•

786. You need to know who to call in
case of an emergency. Besides Mom.

787. You need to know the word
generic can save you a fortune.

•

788. You need to know tanning beds—
surprise!!!—cause skin cancer.

•

789. You need to know that if you make
a habit of eating when you're really happy
or really sad, you're really in trouble.

•

790. You need to know it's more
likely for an overweight person to gain
even more weight than to lose any.

•

791. You need to know that anything
"supersized" is too much food.

•

792. You need to know secondhand
mattresses come with a bonus. Bedbugs.

793. You need to know that
volunteering cures loneliness.

•

794. You need to know that if you
needed ADD medicine in high school,
your employer, fellow employees, and friends
would be grateful if you kept taking it.

•

795. You need to know there's no real
reason for anyone under forty years old to
have anything to do with a plastic surgeon.

•

796. You need to know most of the world's truly
successful people wake up before everyone else.

•

797. You need to know your body will
pay you back for ingesting drinks like Red
Bull to keep the late-night party going.

798. You need to know your ability to eat
sixteen times a day and nap all afternoon without
gaining an ounce will disappear soon. (This is
what happened to your parents.)

•

799. You need to know what pills to take for what.
Antibiotics don't work for relieving a headache.

•

800. You need to know it's easier to keep
nausea and first-aid medicine around before it's
needed rather than drive to the drugstore or your
parents' while barfing out the window.

•

801. You need to know high-fiber food
like fruits and veggies and whole grains
will keep you out of the doctor's office.

802.   You need to know you'll need to deal with stressful issues. Not just hope they'll go away.

•

803.   You need to know you're getting older. Health screenings, checkups, and good hygiene can keep things from going south.

•

804.   You need to know a nice smile will take you farther in life than new clothes. Pick a dentist over a new wardrobe.

•

805.   You need to know flossing helps gums, teeth, heart, and breath.

•

806.   You need to know disinfecting bathrooms, bathtubs, showers, kitchens, handles, and doorknobs every week isn't paranoia. It's why the human race continues to exist.

807.   You need to know to not use the
hospital emergency room for minor stuff.
It takes hours to be seen, costs a small fortune,
and is filled with really sick, toxic people.

•

808.   You need to know green tea is hip.
And comes both caffeinated and decaffeinated.
And reportedly reduces the risk of cancer, heart
disease, cholesterol, and infection. And it's cheaper
than espresso drinks. And at Starbucks.

•

809.   You need to know to not believe
anyone who says, "It's just a cold sore."

810.   You need to know to close the
lid before flushing. Especially if toothbrushes
and washrags are sitting nearby.

•

811.   You need to know to treat any hot tub as
a toxic germ factory. Unless you've personally
cleaned and disinfected it.

•

812.   You need to know to not exercise
in any air you can see. Smog, smoke, and
dust will kill you as fast as inactivity.

You Need to Know the Secrets of Home Repair and Home Depot So When Something Breaks, You Won't Move Home

813. You need to know you won't look like a fool by walking into a Home Depot and announcing you don't know what you need, how to install it, or where it goes. You'll look like a customer.

•

814. You need to know dryer vents holding three pounds or more of lint are a fire hazard. And gross.

•

815. You need to know to regularly examine the shower floor and see if anything on it is mating. Clorox helps here. A year's worth is dirt cheap.

•

816. You need to know how to turn the water off from behind the toilet. You'll want to know this *before* the toilet begins to back up.

817. You need to know to make sure your chimney vents are open before lighting a fire. Smoke needs somewhere to go besides the living room.

•

818. You need to know it's cheaper to get things inspected than to buy new. Plus, Home Depot doesn't sell furnaces or central air conditioning systems.

•

819. You need to know taking home repair classes at Lowe's or Home Depot is like taking shop in high school. Only without the hoods. They teach millions of things like:

How to get organized

How to use power tools

How to install a ceiling fan without doing bodily damage

How to install a new toilet without damaging the house

How to prep and paint interior walls and trim

How to update kitchen cabinets and fixtures

820. You need to know the best way to avoid home repair scams is to never hire anybody who calls you, e-mails you, or shows up at your doorstep. Legitimate companies are too busy working to do these things.

•

821. You need to know that if you don't get approval for planned improvements with your condo association or apartment managers, you can be tossed out on your tush.

822.   You need to know putting off small repairs can have big consequences. Like a hole in the roof that's a fifteen-minute job versus dealing with a flood in the attic that ruins everything and isn't covered by insurance.

●

823.   You should learn there are certain things you never put in the garbage disposal: cantaloupe rinds, eggshells, raw meat, tamale husks. Bird seed isn't recommended either.

●

824.   You need to know that before you do anything to a clogged drain, try a liquid drain opener. It's simple, easy to use, and doesn't involve tools.

825. You need to know to remember
this rule of home repair: good materials are
never cheap, and cheap materials are never good.
Refusal to admit this is why smart people
buy stock in home repair stores.

•

826. You need to know all good repairs start with
a budget and planning. Or a $50 home repair job
can balloon to $500 before the paint dries.

•

827. You need to know a basic truth to home
repair is that it's always twice as expensive as
planned and takes twice as long.

828.   You need to know to have all your
tools and materials together before starting a job.
The alternative is to create a mess, not have the
stuff to fix it, run out of time, live in a pigpen,
call Mom for help, and then move home.

•

829.   You need to know there are times to
call an expert. Like when installing gas lines.
The whole neighborhood will be grateful.

•

830.   You need to know failure to get the required
permits from the local building department means
the most expensive construction can be stopped.

831.   You need to know the best way to never see your contractor again is to pay him in full before the job is finished. Dole it out.

•

832.   You need to know that just by itself, a paint job works wonders for sprucing up a place.

•

833.   You need to know to not spend a fortune on tools. It's better to rent them— and spend a fortune on materials instead.

•

834.   You need to know safety goggles, hard hats, gloves, and nail pouches will help keep you out of the emergency room.

•

835.   You need to know to test your smoke alarm.

836. You need to know a fire extinguisher can keep a small kitchen fire from forcing you to move home.

•

837. You need to know the last thing to use on an electrical fire is water. That's when you run and call 911.

•

838. You need to know that if your circuits are blowing out nightly, it's either the hair dryer or you're living in a firetrap.

You Need to Know How to Buy and Maintain a Car So You Don't Spend $50,000 on a Junker and Have to Move Home

839. You need to know www.carbuyingtips.com can help you get your credit report, secure loan approval, get competing dealer quotes, find the best price on new car warranties, and even help you prepare offer sheets to dealers.

•

840. You need to know to have financing and loan approvals ready before you walk into a dealership. It's called ammunition.

•

841. You need to know that MSRP is the base retail price of a car before all the fees are rolled in. Dealer cost is what the dealer actually paid for the car. The difference is whether the dealer vacations in Maui or Galveston.

842. You need to know to make sure to get an MSRP if you buy the car. It's your guarantee that the features you paid for are actually on the car.

•

843. You need to know the sticker price is fantasyland. Ignore it.

•

844. You need to know buying a good used car can save you thousands of dollars over a new one. Assuming you do your homework and get background checks.

•

845. You need to know to establish your budget before going car shopping. Some hot red sports car could make you forget rent is due on the first.

846.   You need to know there's a price for
being cool. When gas prices rise, it can cost
over $200 a month just to fuel certain cars.

•

847.   You need to know buying a car is like
dating: it's easy to be fooled by looks alone.
Get a vehicle history report at CarFax.com or
ConsumerGuide.com, even on new-looking cars.

•

848.   You need to know to be skeptical
of odometer readings. Someone could make
the car appear barely broken in, when in
reality it was driven into the ground.
Another reason to pull a history report.

849.   You need to know a number of used cars out there have been salvaged, stolen, or recalled. Salespeople may not tell you this. Car histories do.

•

850.   You need to know where the car came from. If it came from the Louisiana or Mississippi coasts, there's a good chance it was flooded. And is worthless.

•

851.   You need to know to not buy any used car before your mechanic puts it on a lift and gives it a full vehicle inspection.

•

852.   You need to know to not argue with the mechanic who finds something wrong with your beloved car. And not to be stupid and buy it anyway.

853.   You need to know what experts think
the car is worth before you buy it. Places to check
are the *N.A.D.A. Official Used Car Guide, Kelly Blue
Book*, or *Consumer Reports Used Car Buying Guide*.
Your friends' opinions are worthless.

•

854.   You need to know to demand a
thirty-day money-back guarantee in writing.
If the dealer says no, leave the car alone.

•

855.   You need to know lenders don't like
people who move a lot. Stay in one place
at least six months before applying.

•

856.   You need to know that 0-percent
financing doesn't apply to everybody.
Only those with good credit scores.

857. You need to know the difference between a three-year loan and a six-year loan can be thousands of dollars in interest.

•

858. You need to know how to compare the difference between low-interest financing and a $3000 rebate. Higher-level math.

•

859. You need to know that at the end of the month, dealers would sell their mother to sell a car. By the end of the year, they're eyeing their firstborn.

•

860. You need to know the secret to buying a hot-selling new car is patience. Car dealers count on a buyer's impatience.

861.   You need to know to leave your
checkbook and credit cards at home when
shopping at a dealer the first time. The dealer's
job is to not let you leave without a car.

•

862.   You need to know four words when
dealing with automobile dealers: get it in writing.
If it's not in writing, as far as the law is
concerned, it was never said.

•

863.   You need to know to not rave about
a car while test-driving it with a salesperson.
The price won't go up, but the pressure to
close a deal that day will.

•

864.   You need to know there's no
such thing as a one-time price to buy a car.
Dealers don't make money turning down
offers they made two weeks earlier.

865. You need to know to never make your trade-in part of the car-buying deal. That's a separate deal. The reason is, dealers can hide hundreds of dollars in fees and markups when the two deals are combined into one.

•

866. You need to know that if your old car is in demand, you can sell it yourself on CarsDirect.com or Cars.com for up to $5000 more than the dealer will pay.

•

867. You need to know to never tell a dealer what you can pay per month. That gives a dealer license to add fees, markups, and profits.

868. You need to know the coolest, newest, never-before-seen cars come with bugs. Wait till the second year to buy. After the bugs are worked out.

•

869. You need to know that when one salesperson leaves and another one comes in, this is the time to go. You're about to be played.

•

870. You need to know that if you don't like to negotiate, you can make an offer to the salesperson and then leave. Let the dealer stew.

•

871. You need to know that if the car is wrecked or stolen, insurance companies don't pay what is owed on the car, but what it's worth. You may owe $18,000 on a car worth only $15,000. That's called "the gap."

872.   You need to know to purchase "gap" insurance if you put less than 20 percent down. Dealers sell gap insurance but it's much, much cheaper at www.gapinsurancequotes.com.

•

873.   You need to know to Google "online auto insurance" and learn the cost of insuring your car before buying it. In many cases, the cost of insurance is the deal killer on that spiffy five-speed sports car.

•

874.   You need to know to buy uninsured motorist coverage. Most of the goobers out there who hit people don't have liability insurance.

875.   You need to know a car lease is just like a car loan: you are obligated to pay it off. You can't just get out of it because your once too-cool-to-live-without convertible has a rattle.

•

876.   You need to know anything longer than a sixty-month car lease is for suckers. At four years things start to break down, warranties expire, car repair gets expensive, and you're still upside-down on the lease.

•

877.   You need to know that when the finance dealer tries to sell you "rust proofing," turn it down.

•

878.   You need to know the $300 "fabric protection" can be duplicated by using two cans of ScotchGuard. Turn it down.

879. You need to know any dealer-prep charges are pure, unearned profit. Turn them down too.

•

880. You need to know the manufacturer's warranty is peace of mind for about 50,000 miles. An extended warranty costs extra, but it's peace of mind for 100,000 miles.

•

881. You need to know to follow the manufacturer's warranty maintenance schedule. It's a minor hassle, but a broken-down car that doesn't qualify for warranty coverage is a huge hassle.

882.   You need to know that no matter
what dealers say, dealers don't sell the best
extended warranties. Actually, dealers don't
sell the best of anything. Except cars.

•

883.   You need to know that if you buy
an extended warranty on a used car, not to
claim anything for sixty days or your file
will be red-flagged. Not fair, but life.

•

884.   You need to know that getting the oil
changed every 4000 miles is what responsible
adults do to keep their cars running smoothly.

You Need to Know How to Get *So* Rich, Your Parents Want to Move in with You

885. You need to know if you use your money to change the world, God will curiously make sure you wind up with more than you need.

•

886. You need to know to put your cash in a money market account, not a CD. The rates are similar, only a CD will charge a fee to take money out.

•

887. You need to know to never fall so much in love with a home that you ignore an inspection's negative findings.

•

888. You need to know where your money is, where it's going, and how to get it. Always.

889.   You need to know one trick of the wealthy is to deposit something from every paycheck into a 401(k). Years later, you'll have a small fortune.

•

890.   You need to know that if an employer offers a matching 401(k) program, that's free money. Every dollar invested automatically doubles.

•

891.   You need to know to invest with your eyes wide open—markets crash, gold dives, real estate tumbles . . . There's no sure thing.

•

892.   You need to know if you start saving in your twenties, you only have to regularly put aside 10 percent of your paycheck to accumulate all the money you'll need for retirement.

893. You need to know people with savings goals reach them. People without goals yank out the credit cards.

•

894. You need to know a fifteen-year mortgage will save you a fortune compared to a thirty-year mortgage.

•

895. You need to know your first financial goal is to accumulate the down payment for a house. Your second goal is to pay off the house.

•

896. You need to know that before buying any real estate, you should get your own broker. Don't use the seller's.

•

897. You need to know financial experts can help. Even the ones on radio and TV.

898.   You need to know buying stocks of large companies and holding them for decades is a time-honored way to accumulate money.

•

899.   You need to know the proven keys to long-term prosperity are making a budget, learning to live without, and regularly giving back to God. Prosperity has nothing to do with a large salary.

•

900.   You need to know that lenders are not your friends. They are cold, hard businesspeople who want their money back. With interest.

•

901.   You need to know wealth is a tool to further God's plans.

You Need to Know What
Gets the FBI and IRS So
Mad at You, You Have to
Hide Out and Move Home

902. You need to know that while you've worked hard for your money, the IRS wants its share. Now.

•

903. You need to know filing too many exemptions is just like stamping your return with a big red "AUDIT ME" stamp.

•

904. You need to know if the IRS doesn't like a certain deduction you've taken, penalties follow.

•

905. You need to know you can go to jail for not declaring income.

•

906. You need to know that if you can't pay your taxes on time, you're toast. You need to work out an installment agreement with the IRS quickly or get a bank loan.

907. You need to know that using pirated software brings the FBI over for a chat. It's against the law.

•

908. You need to know most companies monitor Web surfing. Anything weird will bring the authorities.

•

909. You need to know if you ignore your traffic tickets, the Feds won't come. But the sheriff will.

•

910. You need to know stealing cable signals breaks all kinds of laws. No matter how easy it looks.

You Need to Know God Loves You Even When Nobody Else Does So a Spiritual Crisis Doesn't Cause You to Move Home

911. You need to know God has appointed everyone with special gifts. Even you.

•

912. You need to know eternal truths exist.

•

913. You need to know you'll never learn anything by trusting God only in the easy times.

•

914. You need to know to consider that maybe the world's problems aren't its poor. But its rich.

•

915. You need to know the poor are made in God's image as well. And He has written down specific instructions about the way they are to be treated.

916. You need to know to decide in advance what kind of person you want to be in all situations. Or you'll leave yourself vulnerable.

•

917. You need to know a powerful spiritual tool is to write letters to God.

•

918. You need to know that extending forgiveness is the best way to be good to yourself after someone has been bad to you.

•

919. You need to know that every time we say the Lord's Prayer, we ask God to forgive us *as we forgive others*. Yikes.

920. You need to know to turn over
each business meeting, each relationship,
each dollar to His care. Each day.

•

921. You need to know to not dwell on
your mistakes. There was only one
perfect human being. Move on.

•

922. You need to know to do something wonderful
for somebody every day—and not get found out.

•

923. You need to know *everybody*
is dealing with *something*. Show grace.

•

924. You need to know that it doesn't matter
your job title. You really only have one Boss.

925.   You need to know that doing the
right thing, no matter how costly it seems
at the time, always pays dividends.

•

926.   You need to learn to tithe 10 percent of your
income to a church. The fact that it's not easy is the
point. It's about trusting God that He will provide.

•

927.   You need to know getting knocked
down is no excuse for losing your values.

•

928.   You need to know pride is the biggest
roadblock to forgiveness. And leads to revenge.

•

929.   You need to know to be optimistic.
Christ came to give us hope.

930.   You need to know that hope is a gift
of the Holy Spirit. And when you feel like
you're losing hope, to pray for it.

•

931.   You need to know to not fear change.
It's just evidence God is busy.

•

932.   You need to know to not pass up a chance to
be useful in difficult situations. It's God calling.

•

933.   You should remember who really
owns your body. And to treat it accordingly.

•

934.   You need to know to read your
Bible before walking out the door.

•

935.   You need to know God
will never let you down.

You Need to Know How to
Avoid Getting Sued So You
Don't Have to Spend All
Your Money on Lawyers
and Move Home

936. You need to know it really helps to know an attorney before you need one.

•

937. You need to know to not break any contract with your landlord, your health club, or your banker. Those guys sue.

•

938. You need to know to get everything in writing. It's called proof.

•

939. You need to know to leave everything behind when you resign from a company except for personal files and items. Corporate documents, records, and files belong to the company. And they'll sue.

940. You need to know to treat everyone with courtesy and respect. Even the drunk yelling at you in the bar at 2 a.m. They always have attorneys.

•

941. You need to know to not post anything on the Internet or on a term paper that someone else created without getting permission. Writers sue.

•

942. You need to know to not post compromising pictures of anyone. Embarrassed people sue.

•

943. You need to know to pay back your debts. Especially the ones you were hoping everyone would forget about. Like student loans. The government has battalions of lawyers.

944. You need to know to not start a business
while working for what could be a competitor.
Ex-employers would rather sue than make a sale.

•

945. You need to know spreading
a sexually transmitted disease will result
in lawyers calling. Sick people sue.

•

946. You need to know you can be sued
for delinquent child support. Man or woman.

•

947. You need to know to negotiate
late payments with doctors and hospitals
before attorneys get involved.

948. You need to know to save your paperwork and keep it organized. Save invoices, bills, statements, and tax returns.

•

949. You need to know that often all it takes to avoid a lawsuit is producing a receipt.

•

950. You need to know to keep copies of your really important documents some other place than your bedroom. Like a safe-deposit box.

•

951. You need to know divorce is one long, expensive lawsuit. And the kids always lose.

You Need to Know
to Hold On to Your Ethics
So You Don't Sell Out
and Have to Move Home

952.   You need to know your ethics and values will always be under attack. It's the world we live in.

•

953.   You need to know to never be ashamed of doing the right thing.

•

954.   You need to know the failure of doing what is right will always haunt you.

•

955.   You need to know there is a difference between what is legally permissible and what is ethical.

•

956.   You should always know where the "line" is.

•

957.   You need to know God cares about how you earn your money.

958.   You need to know God doesn't approve of anyone gaining profit by oppressing the poor. Even if 10 percent of the proceeds go to the church.

•

959.   You need to know confidentiality is a key to trusting relationships.

•

960.   You need to know to not accept praise and rewards you haven't earned. Send them in the right direction.

•

961.   You need to know to accept blame when appropriate, not pass it on.

•

962.   You need to know there's no such thing as an ethical dilemma. There's only a decision you don't want to make.

963. You need to know it takes effort to carry and nurse resentments. Forgiveness soothes the soul.

·

964. You need to know to live your life as an example. One day you'll have kids.

·

965. You need to know that if you wait to feel like doing the right thing, the right thing may never get done.

·

966. You should develop the inner strength it takes to stand up and say, "This is wrong." To your friends, to your company, even to your church.

·

967. You should remember God is watching.

You Need to Know How to Act and Think Even More Like an Adult Because the Alternative Will Force You to Move Home

968. You need to know that people
with high self-esteem don't sleep around.

•

969. You need to know that sex is a marriage
sacrament, not a business transaction.

•

970. You need to know betting with the rent
money is high-stakes gambling. Drawing to an
inside straight can bring you home.

•

971. You need to know if your behavior is
secret or abusive, it's only going to get worse.

•

972. You need to know how to deal with difficult
people. Walk away from a fight. Don't ignite it.

973. You need to know your desire for easy
money is how a con artist can pick you clean.

•

974. You need to know it's better to face a
problem head-on. Not with a prescription.

•

975. You need to know that if you are
difficult to get along with, you will have
a hard time keeping a job, keeping friends,
and keeping close relationships.

•

976. You need to know calling someone
over five times a day who doesn't return
your calls makes you appear to be a stalker.

977. You need to know if you're tempted to cheat on your spouse, you'll be tempted to cheat on the next one.

•

978. You need to know to relax someplace besides in a bar.

•

979. You need to know that if you're doing anything on the Internet at 3 a.m., you just might have a problem.

•

980. You need to know how to function in a world that couldn't care less whether you make it in life or not.

981. You need to know to face
problems as they happen. Not put
them off until they're unmanageable.

•

982. You should not be afraid
to make a decision. And stick by it.

•

983. You need to know that instead
of going to your parents for money,
you should work things out. Or do without.

•

984. You need to know that reading a
newspaper, belonging to a church, voting
for a president, and identifying with a
political party are all signs of adulthood.

1001 Things Every Graduate Should Know

985. You need to know that no job, relationship, or situation ever goes according to expectation. Expect to be surprised.

●

986. You need to understand that people who never have to work will never truly believe in themselves.

●

987. You need to know stability doesn't involve changing career plans, lovers, and beliefs every six months.

988. You need to know to not
fear criticism. It's part of life.

•

989. You need to know to go to every wedding
you're invited to. It's a key to building and
honoring lifelong relationships.

•

990. You should never miss a funeral
of a friend or a friend's family.

•

991. You need to know authority
figures are not the enemy.

992. You need to know that a six-figure salary comes with working your butt off in college, then graduate school, and then in the workplace.

•

993. You need to know what's important and what isn't. A plasma TV isn't. Graduate school is. It's called perspective.

•

994. You should put something on your iPod besides music. Sermons, lectures, and books are a start.

995.   You should lower your expectations of
other people, and raise them for yourself.

•

996.   You need to know that if you focus on what's
good today, you'll have a good day. If you focus on
what's bad, the day will go down the toilet.

•

997.   You need to know to listen to gain
understanding, not just enough to offer a flip reply.

•

998.   You need to know that maturity
is the ability to determine future
consequences before making a decision.

999. You need to realize
failure can lead to maturity.

•

1000. You need to know
God isn't finished shaping you.

•

1001. You need to know
to look forward. Not homeward.